Endorsements & Praise

For the *TJ & Dave* show

" ... a creative tour de force, an intellectual high-wire act as astonishing as it is entertaining."

— The New York Times

"BRILLIANT, HEARTBREAKING, MIND-BLOWING, INSPIRING! The best 50 minutes of improv comedy that we've ever seen. But we wouldn't want to insult their effusive skills by speaking so simplistically. Also, it's funny. Drink their Kool-Aid."

— Time Out New York

"The cumulative effect of their spontaneous storytelling is breathtaking ... Without-a-net derring-do brand of theatre."

— NYTheatre.com

"T. J. Jagodowski and Dave Pasquesi step onto a bare stage and, with no prompting or pre-conception, use their brains and bodies to create from whole cloth a one-hour play featuring multiple characters. Their work is often hilarious, sometimes very poignant and always revelatory."

— David Yazbek, The New York Times

" ... a madcap, multi-character, three act comedy was written, cast, opened and closed before our very eyes. It was one of the funniest little plays no one will ever see again."

— The Gothamist

"Run, don't walk, to the *TJ & Dave* Show."

— Chicago Magazine

" ... the two funniest men in North America."

— Charna Halpern, co-founder of iO Theatre,
Geeking Out with ... Charna Halpern

" ... a bunch of us at the show are big fans of *TJ & Dave*. You may have heard of these guys. They improvise an entire, 50-minute, one-act play without stopping to sold-out crowds in both Chicago and New York. Just the two of them—no script, no plan, no audience suggestion—playing all of the characters for almost an hour. It's a feat of theatrical acrobatics (aka 'theacrobatics')."

— *Sean Cole, NPR's Radiolab*

"To improvise short sketches is a skill rather easily mastered. But to successfully improvise a sustained work, with comic text and subtext, over a relatively long period of stage time is a rare, more demanding art. These two actors have mastered this most difficult of improvisational forms with extraordinary success. Now they share what they have learned with fans and practitioners of 'long form' improvisation."

— *Bernard Sahlins, co-founder The Second City*

"One of these guys is the best improviser in the world. And the other one is better."

— *Stephen Colbert*

Improvisation at the Speed of Life

– Special thanks and gratitude to:
Amy Sedaris, Stephen Colbert, Bernie Sahlins,
Kim "Howard" Johnson, J.M. Pasquesi,
and Charna Halpern.

Improvisation at the Speed of Life

T.J. JAGODOWSKI
DAVID PASQUESI
with PAM VICTOR

Solo Roma Inc.
Chicago

IMPROVISATION AT THE SPEED OF LIFE
Published by Solo Roma Inc.
1850 N. Clark Street, Suite 2806
Chicago, Illinois 60614

Original cover art and graphics by J.M. Pasquesi.
Book design by J.M. Pasquesi and Best Design Chicago, Inc.

Improvisation at the Speed of Life
Library of Congress Control Number: 2015931832

Jagodowski, T.J.
Pasquesi, David
Victor, Pam

ISBN-13: 978-0-9773093-3-7
ISBN-10: 0-9773093-3-9

Published by Solo Roma Books, Inc.

10 9 8 7 6 5 4 3 2

Contents

Foreword

by Amy Sedaris

It's been a number of years since I've improvised and many of the rules have been lost to time, but the most fundamental have remained. So when Dave and TJ asked me to write a foreword for their new book about improvisation, without hesitation I said, "Yes," and ... "how long?" After some thought, I quickly added, "Does it pay?" and "Can I get some cash upfront?" Apparently Dave and TJ, the "Grand Poobahs of Improvisation," don't share the same commitment to the rules, because they answered "no", followed by a louder "No!" I guess rules are meant to be broken.

Although I've written a couple of wildly popular picture books, I'm not accustomed to writing forewords to books that contain a lot of words, and from what I can tell, this one appears to have plenty of them. So I consulted my trusty PC where I learned, after typing the words "how to write a foreword to a book," was, "the first place a reader looks when deciding to purchase a book is the foreword." Okay, I suggest that this should not be the first place you look. Why not flip to another section? I mean, any other section, because the fact is, TJ and David have spent years masterfully honing the skills that they have written about in this book. So do you want to judge it by the random scribblings of a person who is not being paid and is probably high?

The next question the foreword should answer, according to the Internet, is, "will this book help me with my problems?" The answer is a resounding "Yes!" Regardless of your situation and or ethnicity, this book will fix it. Maybe reading it will trigger suppressed memories that you haven't acknowledged and for which you have then medicated yourself. One beautiful aspect about improvisation is that there is no need to edit yourself. You can say the first thing that comes to your mind, by the way, let me take a moment here to discuss illiteracy. Three-quarters of a cup of all Americans can't read. And pound for pound, that's the beauty of this book: improvisation! There are no scripts. You make it up as you go along. When you're up there on stage improvising, no one in the audience will ever know that, if it came down to it, you couldn't read the label on a soup can. If I can quote the professional golfer John Daly here, "my wife tried to stab me," and that says everything you need to know about improvisation. Who doesn't want know what happens next?

The most important thing you should take away from this introduction is this: if you are considering reading a book about improvisation, *read this one*, because TJ and David are the best improvisers alive! There are some other good ones, but they're dead now. The point is, this foreword will be ending soon, so while you have the chance, quickly examine the reason you picked up this book. Do you want to be a better improviser? Are you are a fan of *TJ & Dave*? Are you a doctor who is looking for a better way to talk to your patients? Or, do you simply want to learn a new topic, so you have something fresh to say in your carpool? These are all valid reasons to purchase this book.

In closing, I used be in an improv group called the Leftovers. Just thought I should mention it. Where else would I ever have a chance? You can't make this stuff up, but you can in improv. Anything is possible. Say yes, and the whole world opens up. But when you say no, things come to a screeching halt, and that always makes me laugh. The choice is yours. I was just telling my Godson the other day, "Say yes!" He then threw a candy tin and decapitated my five-year-old African violet. Now we're not speaking. Improv!

– *Amy Sedaris*

Introduction

Where We Introduce ...

... David Pasquesi

AND NOW ... A BOOK ABOUT IMPROVISATION. Boy, that sounds like something only an asshole would try to write, doesn't it?

I have great affection for improvisation and the way TJ and I attempt to do it. This book attempts to elucidate our approach to improvisation, and we hope it will be of use to you. We aim to create conditions in which excellent improvisation is more apt to be available to the improviser. But first, we need to identify and name some principles.

I understand the discussion of improvisation is an excellent cure for insomnia and often useful for little else. You may want to make yourself a cup of coffee because we first have to define the things we are going to examine:

> **im•prov•i•sa•tion:** *noun. The act of making something up as it is performed. This term is usually used in the context of music, theater, or dance.*

> **im•pro•vise:** *verb. To fabricate out of what is conveniently on hand.*

The first part of the definition of improvisation begins with "the act of." You see, improvisation is, first of all, an action. It's not a description or an idea, or something we think up. Improvisation is something we *do*.

Secondly, improvisation usually relates to "music, theater or dance." Actors do not have a monopoly on the idea of improvising. Musicians improvise. They respond to the music being played at the moment, without constraints of established melody. Dancers improvise. Poets improvise. Think-tankers improvise. To be specific, this book only discusses improvising onstage as an actor/comedian. Any crossover to other disciplines is coincidental and serendipitous.

We are talking about improvisational theater, which has been around for hundreds of years, since even before the tradition of Commedia dell'Arte (or *Commedia all'improvviso*), a performance of broad, stock character-types improvising around one of several well-known scenarios. They are our forefathers, and we are part of this tradition. We're not re-creating the wheel here. Two guys getting onstage without a script is nothing new.

Returning to our definitions, that of improvisation involves the notion of "making something up." We have reached the point where I fundamentally differ from the dictionary in my definition of this thing. I believe that we are *not* making something up out of thin air. Furthermore, it is most useful to understand that *improvisation* does not mean we are *unprepared*. Otherwise, we'd just call what we do "being lazy."

If we do not know what we are going to say, we should prepare ourselves by knowing all that we possibly can: the issues of the day, our own ideas, and so forth. The best way to prepare for improvisation is to experience life. And think: Think of everything. What do you think about this particular event? This particular point in history? This particular school of thought? What do you think of the fact that you know nothing? You can consider nearly everything if you think enough. You never need to be caught unawares. Thought is part of the preparation, but improvisation is an action. As my teacher once said,

> "The improviser's job is to live an interesting life,
> then tell people about it."
>
> – *Del Close*

Taking one last look at our definitions, to improvise is "to fabricate out of what is conveniently on hand."

Wonderful.

So much easier than creating out of thin air. What's conveniently on hand on an empty stage? Simple: the other person(s) and the communication and trust between you. That is all you have: A blank stage; your partner; your previous experiences and thoughts; and your faith that you will not die tonight, no matter how spectacularly you fail.

Fortunately, that's all you need.

... TJ Jagodowski

I don't know. It seems that the only way to start a book about improvisation is to confess: To admit that I don't know. To fully disclose from the start that, after almost twenty years of its near-exclusive pursuit, the more I discover, the less I know. As I become more aware of situational nuances, technical requirements, and internal understandings, I must acknowledge from the get-go that there are no absolutes in improvisation: There is only elasticity to meet momentary necessities.

With certainty, I believe improvisation is life itself—but a little better. To write about that belief leans to self-help, and I hate the sound of "self-help." Or toward attempts at a novel truly capturing the whole of what it is to live, of which I am, sadly, incapable. Or finally perhaps, a comprehensive human anthology of improvisation, which would suffice if sulfur-breathing, fish-alien overlords came to earth and sought a *Homo sapiens* handbook.

Obviously, I don't yet know what this book is. Honestly, I didn't know where to start. Believing that improvisation is as varied as life itself, how does one describe Everything? Start with rudimentary communication, basic numbers, the beauty of rhythm, the formation of shapes, the very perception of colors, a development of emotional understanding, and the basic physical tasks? You need them all, and you need to master every one of them to improvise.

This book is just what I think about improvisation, and even those thoughts are not mine. My ideas about improvisation were taught to me by folks more and less experienced; by good and rough shows; by family, friends, and strangers on the street; and by the shallowest of self-examinations. I do not know anything about improvisation by myself. I believe improvisation is semi-gifted to us by the mere act of being alive. By caregivers who taught us how to share toys. By the realization that someone else's ideas may be really important. By abandoning assumption and seeking content of character. By punching a bully—intellectually or physically. It is gifted by the ultimate realization of who we are and the knowledge that we will continue to change.

And I believe the rest of an improviser's time is spent logging hours. Doing crap shows where they moved the pool table to give you a stage, you're eleven strong and disturbing people's dinners. Playing to two thousand in a convention hall, jumbotroned and doing crap work, but grabbing the dough equal to a week's pay on your regular job. Sweating balls in a brutally hot rehearsal space without A/C, watching the best scene you've ever witnessed, and realizing you're surrounded by the most creative, dedicated, and lovely group of people you've ever been around in your life. Doing the first show ever for your family or friends and hoping they so get this thing you've been doing for all these years, this thing you can't describe properly to civilians. Hoping that they have the best time and understand the beauty. Then finding a reason for every single show after that to be just as nerve-wracking and captivating and desirous of the same result.

When I first started studying, I pictured Day One as a door. It opened to a hallway—a long one. And on each side were numerous other doors. Each time I felt I'd learned something, I opened another door, revealing a brand new hallway, just as long and with just as many new doors. And this happened over and over and again. For a long time, these endless hallways of infinite doors were maddening to me. How will I ever finish? When will I learn it all? When will I be good?

I don't know exactly the day or time when this feeling not only evaporated, but was replaced with a great comfort in knowing with certainty this journey, this relationship, would never end. The endless hallways and infinite doors meant she would never leave me. We will never be done together, and we'll never get bored with each other, as long as my energy and desire met her variety and depth.

I do know this. I may never get good, but I can spend a lifetime getting better. I don't know when exactly I knew what it meant to me to be an improviser. It must have been the day I fell in love with it because love is sure what it feels like to me.

A KEY AND A CAVEAT

This book is not normal. The format may take some getting used to, so if you want to understand it better, read this little chapter. Most people will skip over it because they have no impulse-control and they want to jump into the meat of the book. They're not reading this part, so we can feel free to talk about them. Go ahead. Take a moment to feel a little superior.

 Unless otherwise noted, the views represented in this book belong to David Pasquesi and TJ Jagodowski.

Pam Victor introduces each chapter and then turns it over to us (TJ and David). Further, her clarifications and interjections show up in italicized form to differentiate her voice from ours. You'll also meet Pam in the interview-styled "In Conversation" segments. These interludes spotlight one element of a topic and are in script format—a style that we sometimes find more accessible. They are meant to invite you into our conversations about improvisation, giving you a fly-on-the-wall feeling. If you truly want to be part of those conversations, you are welcome to chime in with your own witty rejoinders, insightful thoughts, and biting comebacks. However, since we are bound by time and space, you will not be able to actually participate in our conversations.

The stuff in this book is what we think about improvisation and what has served us well, individually and as *TJ & Dave*. Only you can be the judge of what works best for you, so take the helpful bits and use the rest to roll up a fat one. From shortform games to the most complicated, newest longform structure, we hold a great deal of respect for all forms of improvisation, but we are devoting these pages mainly to talking about what we know best and practice in *TJ & Dave*, a two-person, longform improvisation.

Our show is unusual in its structure. It's just the two of us and we get about fifty minutes. We understand you might not necessarily have the luxury of as much time as we do. We are not going to be tagged-out in two minutes (or ever). A third person isn't going to walk into our scene to "improve" it. We're not going to get the hook at twenty-three minutes because we're on the bill with three other groups. Though we will share our thoughts on other structures toward the end of the book, we figure it's best if we stick to discussing improvisation as we perform it in our show. Hopefully you'll find some principles in here that apply to all improvisation, and perhaps you'll be able to take some of this stuff and use it in your own work.

We also want to say straight out that we're talking about ideals here. They are goals toward which we aim. We don't hit these marks every time. Sometimes we don't even land on the target. But over the course of our time together, we've come up with some ideals on which we've set our sights. You are holding these ideas and ideals in your hands.

PART ONE

THE EARLY YEARS

1

PATHS TO IMPROVISATION

Nowadays, improvisation has its own culture where lessons and legends are passed down from teacher to student and peer to peer in classes, workshops, and at the bar after a show. We all learn from the community of improvisers. Many students in Chicago are learning from teachers who learned directly from Del Close, widely considered one of the originators and most powerful advocate of longform improvisation. And it was Viola Spolin and her son, Paul Sills, who heavily influenced Del.

The paths that led David and TJ to improvising are as individual as they are, but both performers are members of that same culture where learning, teaching, and performing are all part of the journey.

David and TJ believe there are a rare few original thinkers in improvisation, and they certainly don't count themselves among that elite group. They are clear to point out that whatever they've achieved is a result of those who have come before them, in addition to the many they have stood beside onstage. "Though we couldn't get close to crediting everyone who has taught us about improvisation," David says, "we're going to take a shot at hitting the biggest targets. Tell the stories of the often-fortuitous series of events that lead us here, and where we are today is on that same path."

David's first exposure to improvisation stemmed from his mother's desire to get him out of the house. She practically insisted he accompany his older brother to an improvisation class at The Player's Workshop, which was then affiliated with The Second City and was the only official school of improvisation at the time.

HOW'D DAVID GET HERE?

I tagged along with my brother Tom, who was then in law school. (I was pursuing a B.A. in not-anything-like-theater.) For some reason, even though the class was full, the teacher, Judy Morgan, let me take it without registering. I loved it from the start. While taking the first classes, I read Jeff Sweet's *Something Wonderful Right Away*. My teacher was in there! Turns out Judy was in one of those amazing Second City casts, where she performed with Harold Ramis, Brian Doyle-Murray, Joe Flaherty, John Belushi, and Eugenie Ross-Leming. She was a great teacher and made it easy for me to love improvisation from the get-go. I went through that series of classes, which culminated in an original revue show on the Mainstage of Second City one Sunday afternoon. That was my first time in front of an audience. I was about 20 years old. And it was wonderful.

I went back to finish college, never considering improvisation as a possible career for me—or anyone else, for that matter. The following year, I was sitting on an airplane bound for Rome on a yearlong study-abroad program. This guy walked by carrying Hunter S. Thompson's *The Great Shark Hunt*. I told him I was a fan of the book. We started talking. He said his name was Joel. We started drinking. We started joking around and making trouble. By the time the plane landed, they were out of beer and we were fast friends, soon to be roommates.

> *The new buddies hung out a lot in Rome, traveling together, running around, and occasionally busking on street corners, where Joel would sing and David would juggle. They even performed in the school's talent show. Now and then, the two would joke about working at Second City when they returned to Chicago.*

"*He said 'joke,'*" David clarified, "*because, at the time, working in improvisation and comedy seemed like a silly pipe dream. But Joel had some brothers who performed at the Second City, so we thought, maybe it isn't that silly after all.*" *David's partner-in-crime was Joel Murray and his brothers are the aforementioned Brian Doyle-Murray and Bill Murray.*

Upon returning to the States, David resumed the business of finishing college and getting a "real" job, after a slight detour as a cowboy on an 88,000 acre sheep ranch in southwest New Mexico. He figured commercial real estate was where he was headed in life, and he'd been accepted at the Kellogg Business School at Northwestern. David tells what happened next:

Just as I was about to complete the registration, I made a drastic decision to blow off grad school and, instead, live on a buddy's floor and work for him as a laborer. I'm sure you can imagine how thrilled my parents were.

Joel and I started to perform together a little when he got some advice from his brothers. They told him to find a guy named Del Close and to study with him. We did just that. We found him. (Joel did all the practical work of finding him. I had no idea who any of these people were.) So there I was again, trotting along behind a guy, finding my way to improvisation, with no end goal in mind other than the inkling that it seemed to be the next thing to do. Joel and I ended up at a workshop at CrossCurrents on Wilton Street in Chicago. Del had us audition that night in front of the class, to see if we were good enough to join them. I remember we did a scene that turned out to be about two guys coming-to in an apartment the morning after a big party.

> *They were allowed to join the class. In fact, Del let them both take it for half-price.*

That workshop had been going on for a few weeks. Del was using the group to work out a form of improvisation that would be, in itself, the entertainment, rather than merely a means to develop material. Second City was pretty much the only game in town; and though they used improvisation to develop material, the show for which they sold tickets was a scripted revue. In fact, to this day, you can get into the improvisation sets for free at Second City.

Del's dissenting opinion was that improvisation could be consistently good enough to be more than just a means to an end. Del thought improvisation alone could be worthy of the ticket price. So it seemed that Joel and I had wandered into the class Del was using as guinea pigs for some of these ideas.

 The *Harold* is the basic structure of longform group improvisation from which many other longform structures have sprung. Today, nearly every improvisational comedy theater in the United States has at least one Harold show. (For more information about Del Close and the Harold, you should check out Kim "Howard" Johnson's book, *The Funniest One in the Room*.)

In the workshops, we found that longer improvised scenes tended to wander and meander, to transform into other scenes. It was often very fluid and trippy and fun, but not all that cohesive. Del was trying to formulate a more defined and watchable structure within which we could improvise—a way to investigate a theme through scenes, games, and monologues. And so, Joel and I ended up in the workshops that Del was using to formalize a method of using the Harold to create a fully improvised show an audience would pay to see.

DAVID AND DEL

Using the two-person scene as the mainstay of the Harold, Del had us get up on our feet and try to make a story out of disparate scenes that somehow connected to a central topic, which was based on an audience suggestion. There was a lot of trial and error. In fact, at first there was mostly error. After a while, the trial yielded something other than errors. Eventually, after a great deal of experimentation, we arrived at the structure commonly used today. (We'll go into more detail about how we approach the Harold if you care to stick around awhile.)

Personally, I found the two-person scenes to be the most lovely. They were usually pretty good because Del taught us to simply react with honesty, and that seemed to be enough. Others may have told me before, but I first understood it with Del. He was not asking us to be funny or entertaining, but merely honest—and, hopefully, interesting. I remember Del saying, "You don't have to be afraid to tell the truth. No one will believe you think that way. They'll think you're acting."

During those months of workshops upstairs at CrossCurrents, I learned many lessons from Del that I still employ each time I take the stage decades later. Del taught us to play slowly without worrying about entertaining the audience. He stressed the importance of playing at the top of our intelligence. He instructed us to play characters close to ourselves, "as a thin veil," and to respond honestly to the scene and the other players. Another big lesson I took from Del was not to talk too much because overusing words diminishes the power of each one. Del taught us to dare to be poets.

Del also would reprimand us for trying to get a laugh because that was not constructive in these scenes or for the Harold. He would remind us that good improvisers are not going for laughs; they are going for cheers. He said that little laughs along the way would only dissipate the big reaction. We were taught to let it build, whatever it was. Be patient, so that when a response from the audience finally did come, it would be huge. That one really stayed with me.

WORKING THE HAROLD

Boy, did we do a lot of shows back then. A lot of not very good shows too. At that time, a show would consist of three Harolds in a night, each from a different team, and the audience would then vote on the "winner" for the evening. Even when performing, we still experimented: with different openings, with different group games, even with the notion of an outrider or narrator who did not participate as a player in the scenes but served more as a director sitting on the sidelines shaping the story by cutting off or setting up scenes. In the end, we found it more elegant to do that work from within the show itself.

Most of the time, we had no idea if we were doing what we were supposed to be doing because we had no idea what this thing was supposed to look like. None of us had seen a Harold. Nevertheless, on occasion, we would get the feeling that all was going perfectly. Seamlessly. Effortlessly. Sometimes it felt as though we knew what was going to happen next, and there seemed to be no need to make choices because it was all so clear as to how it would unfold. When that happened, we used to say, "Harold was here tonight." I think we said that because it sounded cool and mystical, but it was also true. We felt like something other than us was at work. And that feeling—that very same feeling—is what I still try to experience today when I step onstage with TJ. Though now I know, it is not merely something that capriciously happens to us.

> *Back then, before ImprovOlympic became iO and moved into its permanent theater, there were only a couple of teams at first, mostly made up folks who were not interested in becoming full-time actors. One of the first Harold troupes was The Baron's Barracudas. At the outset, it included Joel Murray, Chris Barnes, Kim "Howard" Johnson, Mark Beltzman, JJ Jones, Tara Gallagher, and (briefly) Jack Wells.*

 CrossCurrents was the building owned by Tom Goodman. It was a bar and cabaret where Del taught class. ImprovOlympic was the company that Charna had with David Shepherd. (We never referred to it as ImprovOlympic, only as CrossCurrents.) ImprovOlympic moved from CrossCurrents to many other venues, where they held classes and did nights of Harold shows. It was a gypsy company until the Wrigleyville address.

Charna Halpern, co-founder of iO, split Joel and I up. She put me on a team of mostly stand-up comedians, which included Jeff Jenna and Joey Gutierrez, because I did stand-up back then as a way to get more stage time and to become a better improviser. The stand-up team was soon disbanded, and I was added to the Barracudas. Around the same time, Honor Finnegan joined the group. And boy, was she great.

> *Much of the team also performed at Gaspars (now Schuba's Tavern) in a team called* Harold Be Thy Name. *Eventually, Second City came to see a show there, and they hired four of the five males. David was the fifth. He continued to attend Del's class and once a week a group of them would still trot down to perform at Gaspars with a new collection of players: Honor Finnegan, Becky Claus, John Judd, Steve Burrows, Bill Russell, Judy Nielsen, and Brian E. Crane.*

Along with Howard Johnson, we also continued to be the house team at CrossCurrents, which meant we performed on every show night—I think that amounted to twice, then later three times a week. We tried to get onstage a lot. And when we weren't doing shows, we'd go watch the set at Second City with Jim Fay, Meagen Fay, Isabella Hoffman, Dan Castellaneta, Richard Kind, and Mike Hagerty. ... a great group of folks. The way things turned out, I got to stay at CrossCurrents and study with (and be reminded by) Del for almost one more year. I certainly would have preferred to be hired at Second City at the same time as my friends. Like most of the things that turn out to be great for me, I never would have chosen that path.

Eventually, I was hired at Second City, performed in the touring company, and was in the original cast of their Second City Northwest theater. I moved to the Second City Mainstage in 1988. While I was there, Bernie Sahlins stepped down as director, so we needed a replacement. Joel and I went into Joyce Sloane's office and suggested Del direct us. He hadn't worked at Second City for many years, but somehow it all came together. I ended up in *The Gods Must Be Lazy*, directed by Del in a cast with a few other folks from CrossCurrents, including my buddy Joel (Murray), Tim Meadows, Chris Farley, Joe Liss, Holly Wortell, and Judith Scott.

Around 1990, I left Second City after doing four revues, including *Flag Smoking Permitted in Lobby Only* and *It Was Thirty Years Ago Today*. Soon afterward, I started doing plays in Chicago, and even shared the stage with my mentor, Del, in *The Chicago Conspiracy Trial* and *Del and Dave in Rehearsal for the Apocalypse*.

TRANSITIONAL '90s

As I became busy with scripted acting, I found myself improvising less and less. Now and then when I was in L.A., I did some Harolds at Jeff Michalski and Jane Morris' place, Upfront Comedy Theatre, in Santa Monica.

> *At the time, regulars there included Joel Murray and other folks from Chicago, as well as the gang from Toronto, which included Colin Mochrie, Ryan Stiles, and Deb Theaker. Even veterans like Paul Dooley would sometimes play.*

I also did a show at The Annoyance Theatre for about a year called *Moe Green's Other Eye*, which involved both sitting around talking and improvising scenes. I did some improvised monologue shows with Joe Bill at the Annoyance too, and *Combo Platter* with Jeff Garlin. But for the most part, by the late '90s, I had stopped improvising regularly. Few of my old friends were around, most having left for the coasts in search of more remunerative employment. I also noticed that the kind of improvisation being done at that time didn't seem too familiar or interesting to me. Nowhere in Chicago (including the stuff I was doing at the time) did I find the kind of improvisation that we used to pursue with Del.

And then Del died.

Besides that first class with Judy Morgan, the only person I ever really studied improvisation with was Del. He taught me all that I know and more than I'll remember. He was my major professional influence. And he was my friend. The day before he died, I visited him in the hospital to say goodbye. I remember that Del told to me to continue to do the kind of improvisation that he had taught me. He also said, "Keep this stuff going." And though I thought that seemed a reasonable request, I knew I had to find other folks interested in the same ideas and pursuits. I don't think I consciously set out to honor Del's request. Even so, on some level, I somehow kept taking steps in that direction. And I kept my eyes open.

At the second Chicago Improv Festival in 1999, just a month after Del's death, I had an opportunity to do a show with Mick Napier, with whom I hadn't improvised in about a decade, and Scott Adsit, with whom I had never improvised. We just got up onstage and started performing without any discussion of what we were going to do. I did the show because it seemed like an interesting next thing to do. It ended up being enough fun that I did another show at the next CIF. Then at the festival in 2001, there was a pickup show thrown together at the last minute because they needed some players to fill in, so I joined them.

That group included a few guys I had known a long time, and TJ Jagodowski, whom I had only met once or twice.

> *So how did TJ find his way to the 2001 Chicago Improv Festival and what catalysts set him on his path to improvisation? Here's TJ:*

TJ'S PATH TO IMPROVISATION STARTED ON A NEWLYWED'S COUCH

In its most basic sense, how I came to improvisation is far from interesting and even farther from unique. My friend took me to a show, and I was hooked. It is the same story for ninety percent of my improvising friends. If my history is intriguing at all, it is because of the people I was lucky enough to watch play, be taught by, harass with questions, or with whom I became friends. Folks along the way who were kinder to me than I deserved, and believed in me far more than any of my achievements warranted have also defined it for me. It's hard not to be transformed after seeing one's first revue at Second City.

I grew up in Holyoke, Massachusetts, a city I love to my bones. It is an old mill town, not unusual to the northeast that saw its heyday at a time when paper and textile productions were at their height. It has struggled for many years with poverty, a large drug trade, and general lack of opportunity. I would never have wanted to grow up anywhere else. But with the problems that Holyoke faced, an arts scene was not high on the civic list of priorities. I was exposed to little theater, had never heard of improvisation, and had no designs on being a performer when I arrived in Chicago in 1993. Then came that one night when that friend took me to see a revue at Second City called *Take Me Out to the Balkans*. It was a biblical moment—a Cecil B. DeMille *light-parts-the-clouds-and-a-beam-of-heaven-hits-you-in-the-noggin* moment, an *if-you-don't-try-this-and-do-what-they're-doing-you-may-never-be-happy* kind of moment. And as epic as it felt, it is this moment that happened to the other ninety percent of the folks I know, whether at Second City or another theater.

Years after this experience, while I was touring with Second City down in Charleston, South Carolina, I got to meet Stephen Colbert, who was in the *Balkans* show. I told him about being in the audience and how I felt transformed and that it made me want to try doing this stuff.

He said, "*That's Catch 27 for me.*"

I walked away thinking, "What an asshat. I'm the 27th person who said that to him? And why did he say it with a sentimental smile? That's a special kind of mean."

A few days later, I went back home to Chicago. I had kept my job working at the box office at Second City while I toured, because you never knew how many shows there would be in any given month or when they would invite you to no longer be a part of the touring group. I was dallying while bringing the outgoing mail upstairs to be stamped, staring at the Bill Utterback drawings of past shows and casts that hung in the hallways. And I got it, all of a sudden. There, under one of the drawings, was a show title: *Catch 27*. Mr. Colbert had had the same experience. We, not he and I, but we "Second Citizens" and Chicago improvisers, each had that moment when we saw the thing that grabbed us and wouldn't let go.

Let's back up a second. It was the encouragement of a good friend that got me to start classes at Second City after seeing that first show. Eventually, I got that job in the box office, and got to sneak into the shows where I watched Mr. Colbert and Mr. Carell; took class with Don DePollo, Marty de Maat, Michael Gellman, and Norm Holly; drew a paycheck in one sense or another from Bernie Sahlins, Joyce Sloane, Andrew Alexander, and Kelly Leonard;

eavesdropped on rehearsals with Scott Adsit and Tina Fey; understudied with Jim Zulevic, Brian Stack, and Rachel Dratch; picked the brains of and laughed with Horatio Sanz and Jerry Minor; got show notes from Sheldon Patinkin; performed in casts with Tami Sagher, Sue Gillan, Al Samuels, Holly Walker, Dave Pompeii, and Stephnie Weir; did the first post 9/11 revue with Andy Cobb, Sam Albert, Keegan-Michael Key, Jack McBrayer, and Abby Sher; and was mentored in so many things by Kevin Dorff.

In time—and, I believe this to be a matter of the way Chicago goes about its business and fun—I got to be friends with all of them. I wanted to mention these folks by name to highlight the outrageous amount of talent to which I was fortunate enough to be exposed. These folks were just wandering about the scene. You could turn a corner and bump into one of the most amazing improvisers who ever lived. The very best part is that they were also some of the sweetest and most generous people you could meet, not only with their talent but their time, their knowledge, and their friendship. I have never known another city or another field of interest as sharing and supportive as folks pursuing comedy in Chicago.

And we haven't scratched the surface of the ImprovOlympic yet. My friend took me to my first show at iO and it happened again. Red Sea parts. Bush burns. Trumpets blare. Tuna melts fall from the sky. (One man's manna and all.) It wasn't until I saw longform that I truly realized what improvisation could be. It was group-based. Essentially cooperative. Scenically cohesive. Explorative and wide of the mind. A short while after seeing my first show, a few friends from Second City and I put up a show in the iO's space upstairs. Charna Halpern came to check it out, and afterward she gave me a scholarship to take classes for free (and a large example of someone's generosity and belief in me beyond my achievement).

As with Second City, I was exposed to an even larger pool of the most talented, intelligent, and interesting people. I was taught by Craig Cackowski, Peter Gwinn, Noah Gregoropoulos, and Charna. I watched *The Upright Citizen's Brigade* and *Jane* and *Trio* play; was inspired by and included in projects by Bob Dassie; and got to be part of *J.T.S. Brown, Atlantis,* and *Armando Diaz.* Some of these names may not mean anything to folks outside of my age in Chicago, but to me they meant the world. I learned how to treat a young improviser because of Rich Talarico. I played with, laughed with, wrote with, and became best friends with Jack.

It was during this time that I was exposed to The Annoyance Theatre, its philosophies, and folks like Mick Napier, Mark Sutton, Joe Bill, Eddie Furman, and Susan Messing. And again, my improvising life was changed for the better. They strengthened my voice and made me feel surer on my feet.

I cannot overemphasize what an amazing time and place Chicago was then and still is now. We nerds, stoners, goths, and the otherwise disenfranchised found a series of pathways to tree houses with our favorite soda, books, and toys. Shamans, yogis, and wizards told us that we weren't supposed to hide our oddities, passions, and idiosyncrasies anymore. We were beak-fed beliefs and told we could fly with only that. And the community rose to make that all true. Those who wanted it and could see it for what it was, we were given a home.

Most of the names aforementioned are well known to most folks familiar with improvising. They are mentioned specifically because it's more satisfying to hear a name you recognize than one you don't. But I have learned as much if not more from people you've likely never heard of, folks like Paul Grondy, for one. And I still do, on a daily basis. I am lucky in that I can tell most of them that on any given day because we still play together and drink soda in the same tree houses.

There is one name that even fans of improvisation mostly likely will not have heard. Her name was Lisa Haleski. She changed it for legal reasons; I believe it had something to do with falling in love with a guy and marrying him. We met while attending Syracuse University. When she graduated, she moved to Chicago. I had studied TV/radio/film production. By the time I graduated, Lisa was working on the TV show *The Untouchables*. When I told Lisa that I was thinking of moving to Chicago, she said I could crash with her, and she might be able to put in a word for me at work. What she did was, as a newlywed, she let me sleep on her couch for six months. And she got me a job as a production assistant on the TV show. Then she determined the course for the rest of my life. It was she who brought me to Second City, she who told me to take classes. She who brought me to iO. She who encouraged and inquired with each step I took.

Lisa is not an actress or an improviser. She is a friend. And I wish a Lisa on any one of you; a person who sees a thing in you that you never saw. Who believes strongly enough that it starts to make you believe too. Who has nothing to gain for what they want for you except your happiness. With the exception of the gang I share bloodlines with, Lisa has done more than anyone to make me what I am today. I am eternally grateful to her for showing me the tree houses, for introducing me to the similarly damaged, for not taking "I don't know about this" for an answer. If you have a Lisa in your life, listen to her. If not, find one. She will show you the thing that makes it rain tuna melts.

2

THE BIRTH OF *TJ & DAVE*

As the story goes, at a celebration of the 95th birthday of the great cellist Pablo Casals, a reporter asked him why he still practiced five hours a day. Mr. Casals answered, "Because I think I'm finally making progress."

Though TJ and David both claim their first *TJ & Dave* show in 2002 was rough, they gave it another shot the following week. They've been giving it a shot ever since, almost every Wednesday night—at the iO Theater in Chicago and, currently, in their own Mission Theater in iO's extraordinary new complex. More than a decade later, they say they seem to be "finally making progress."

TJ was added to the Second City's Mainstage cast around 1998, and it was during that time that he first met David.

TJ ON MEETING DAVE

Any improviser who had been around for a few years knew the name Dave Pasquesi. He had a sort of Sasquatch mystique to him. All of us had heard of him, a few claimed to have seen him, but we had very little physical evidence to go on. Then one night, there he was in the audience. On most nights at Second City, after the written sketch show there would be "the set," an improvised third act when we could invite any guest to join us. We invited David. And he said yes.

 This was during the 1998-99 show *The Psychopath Not Taken* with Kevin Dorff, Rich Talarico, Stephnie Weir, Susan Messing, and Tami Sagher.

Backstage, we drew straws to see who would get to play with Bigfoot. Everyone wanted to get his or her hands on him, but Tami drew the winning straw, the only one of us who would get to play with Dave. They did a very patient scene together where they played a couple for whom each room of the house brought out a different emotion. For example, the kitchen made them angry, the bathroom horny ... you know, that sort of thing.

Watching it, I started to understand better the things people said when describing Dave—his stillness and focus and listening. It was a slowly developing scene, but there was never a sense of anxiousness or hurry. Dave didn't rush a thing. Everything was discovered as it went. Dave just stood still and listened until the next thing presented itself.

Later that night, I told Dave it was nice to meet him. I called him "Mr. Pasquesi." I meant it honestly as a sign of respect. He laughed. And I didn't see him again for a good while.

> *Their second meeting was at an early Chicago Improv Festival in 2001, thanks to an imminent writers' and actors' strike. The festival had planned on featuring some improvisers employed by Saturday Night Live, MadTV, and Conan, that would have been available during a strike. When the strike didn't happen, the festival producers suddenly found themselves short of players. Calls went out to the people who were in town and were unemployed for non-strike-based reasons. TJ found himself performing that night with Kevin Dorff, Scott Adsit (both had cleared their schedules for the festival), Mick Napier, Jimmy Carrane ... and David Pasquesi.*

As a habit, I am a nervous performer and David had some anxieties that night as well. We stood in the wings together before the show, talking about meditation and hoping to calm ourselves. The show went pretty well. As part of the festival's promotional material, we all were interviewed in a basement room afterward. David, who hadn't been improvising on any regular basis at that point, was asked how he felt about playing that night. He said, "I would do this all the time if this group was in it ... it's great fun."

At that moment, Scott Adsit and I perked up like a pair of RCA Victor dogs, catching each other's eyes. As soon as the interview was over, Adsit cornered me in the hall and said, "I get first shot at Pasquesi. Don't cockblock me on this." He meant it jokingly, but not entirely. At the time, Dave was spending more time in L.A., and he and Scott ended up doing some stuff out there. It would be some time before Dave and I met again.

Then one night, I was hanging out at the bar at iO with my friend Noah Gregoropoulos, who is the closest thing to a guru iO has had since Del's passing. Out of nowhere, Noah said he thought Dave and I would be an interesting pair onstage. At the time, I wanted to do just about every show

I could. (I'm still like that now.) So somehow I got past my nerves and picked up the phone.

I asked Dave if he was interested in playing. He said he was doing a play at the time but that we should talk when the run ended. That play was *Glengarry Glen Ross* at the Steppenwolf Theatre, one of Chicago's most highly esteemed theaters. I went to the show to see what Dave was like, to check him out. I thought if we were going to work together, catching the show would be a friendly thing to do. And being at Steppenwolf, chances are it would be a great show just to see. Dave was playing Ricky Roma, and, God was he good. It's a big, bold part, and Dave completely owned it. I thought, "Holy Christ, what have I gotten myself into?" He seemed so large and intimidating, and I was very worried that I wouldn't be able to hold a stage with him.

> *Both TJ and David are equally fuzzy on what followed. Neither remembers who made the next phone call or the majority of content in their myriad conversations, which often took place at a coffee shop called Savories that used to be in Old Town. Both were clear on the few rules for their show. They wouldn't take audience suggestions. They wouldn't add new cast members until needed or until they got the show into a shape where it didn't feel like they were adding bodies to a sinking ship. They would let improvisation guide them.*

All those things are still true.

David corroborates the duo's first meeting at the Second City. He had seen TJ in the revue, and thought he was very good. David recalls the improvised set with Tami afterward:

It was a scene that took place in various rooms of a house, and when we would change rooms, we would change the tone of the scene. We hadn't planned on doing that, but we both noticed it and continued doing it. Backstage, after the show, this punk called me "Mr. Pasquesi" and I thought, "Fuck you, kid." (I was more taken aback and amused at being called "Mister.") That was about 15 years ago, maybe more. Then TJ stopped doing scripted material. I knew that he had some trouble with balance or vertigo.

In 2001, we did that show for the Chicago Improv Festival at the Athenaeum Theatre, and most of the seats were full. I hold a high regard for improvisation, and I believe an improviser has a responsibility to take the stage with consciousness and intent. It was the largest audience I was aware of for longform improvisation, and I didn't want them to think improvisation is uninteresting (or worse), so I very much wanted to *not* be terrible. TJ and I spoke before the show. I remember we were standing stage right.

TJ seemed very kind and very bright. His love for improvisation was obvious. He viewed it as I did, as more than being funny or clever. From the start, TJ and I have shared the same high regard and respect for improvisation that we have to this day.

Towards the end of that show, I started a scene waaaaay downstage at the very lip of the stage—toes hanging over a very deep orchestra pit. (That's something I like to do if an audience might intimidate me: Walk right up into their face ... follow the fear.) I believe the scene was on the window ledge of a tall building. So we were doing this scene, and out walked TJ, the guy who has trouble with balance and vertigo. He stood on the edge of a long fall. During the scene, but *sotto voce* between us, I asked, "What are you doing out here?"

He grinned a little and said something like, "This is where the scene is."

I liked him.

As it turned out, I didn't gain traction with Scott Adsit. He was in Los Angeles, and I was in Chicago. We tried to write some sketches together via email, but never performed any of them. I still wasn't improvising regularly at that point because I just didn't have anyone in Chicago to play with who shared my kind of performing attitude. So when TJ called, I decided to give it a shot. We seemed to be on the same page about improvisation.

As TJ said, we don't remember the details of our first phone calls, but we met a couple times for coffee to talk about the show we wanted to do. I wanted to offer an example of another kind of improvisation, something different than what we often saw at that time, which tended to be a lot of faster, funnier, and cleverer improvisation. I didn't see many longer, slower, more honest or organic scenes. We thought we'd give that a try. (I am not particularly good at the faster, funnier variety of improvisation; I believe there is room in improvisation for all kinds, but that's not the type I do.) TJ was willing to try this experiment with me, and I knew he was more than capable. There are many good improvisers, and most of them have no interest in doing the kind of show we do—or at least they didn't in 2002. Back then, there was only TJ.

We made a commitment to attempt improvisation based on what Del assured us would be enough: to respond honestly, moment to moment, and trust that the rest will take care of itself. We deliberately did not come up with a structure. You could say we decided to improvise the way we would improvise.

The whole prospect was terrifying. I had no desire to go up on a Wednesday night and suck, which was (and still is) a very real possibility.

I was keenly aware that:

> TJ and I didn't know one another.
> We were taught in different ways.
> We weren't and still aren't the same ages.
> We don't have similar backgrounds or life experiences.
> All the guys I came up with, myself included, were mostly goofballs or fuckups, and TJ is not like that at all.

Those are all the reasons it shouldn't have worked. And then after our first show together at the iO, we had other reasons.

> *At this point, David and TJ asked Charna for a regular time slot at iO Theater, and they inherited a two-person show late Wednesday nights.*

Charna gave us the place. She was (and is) very gracious. We could have anything we wanted. She even offered us more popular time slots, like weekends. But we wanted an off-show time so that we could start quietly, and then maybe move to a weekend when we got better.

We are still on Wednesdays late night, but in our own theater space called The Mission.

> *They had a regular show time, but they still needed to find an audience. TJ admits he has expertise with neither technology nor design, but he made a couple handwritten signs on notebook paper and pinned them up in the theater bathrooms. That was the entire scope of advertising for their first show. As it turned out, they ended up with a nice house. TJ recalls that first venture like this:*

There was certainly a buzz going about Dave coming back to play. Everyone had heard stories about him, and here was a chance to see him play in our (iO) sandbox.

Trust us, this is all made up.

We did a few things that first night that we have done every time since— and one thing we would never do again. We went up onstage halfway through a song by Dave's friend's band, The Ike Reilly Assassination. We milled about the stage for the remainder of the song, and then we introduced ourselves. Since we weren't taking a suggestion, we asked people to, "Trust us, this is all made up." We have done these things every show since.

The thing we would never do again was completely, irrevocably, and intensely suck. We have had less than stellar shows since, but nothing like that first show. We were horrible. We tanked. We *80-gallon-saltwater-tropical-fish aquarium* tanked. We *Houdini-upside-down-with-a-burst-appendix-in-water* tanked. We *lone-student-in-Tiananmen-Square* tanked. We were not good.

Our first scene took place at a bus stop. I'm sure it was no more than twenty minutes long, but it felt like it took up most of 2002. Two guys were waiting for a bus ... that's almost all that I remember. The rest is a miasmic swirl. There was wristwatch checking. There was unconnected dialogue. There was unfocused character play. It was a gloomy mess. All of which led to Dave turning to me and saying, "I'm bored." At that moment, I was unsure as to whether he had spoken to me as "Man 1 Waiting for Bus" or Dave Pasquesi, improvisational partner. It would have been an appropriate line from either.

> *David points out that the partners did not know one another at all. They didn't hang out, and they didn't come up together. Aside from that one group show at the Chicago Improv Festival, all they had done was get together a couple times and talk about deliberately not having any parameters for what they were going to try. Then they tried it and, as David says, " ... nothing was happening. Nothing good anyway."*

I said something like, "I'm bored. I don't want to be here anymore." So TJ asked what or where I would like to be, and I said something like, "I want to be an astronaut." We ham-handedly transformed the location to a space shuttle. (They were still running back then. For future readers with no understanding that Americans once had a place in the world beyond our atmosphere: a space shuttle was a low earth orbital spacecraft used predominantly to ferry astronauts to and from the International Space Station or to repair the Hubble Space Telescope.) Unfortunately, the change to the spacecraft location was not helpful. Turned out, I didn't want to be there either.

Man, that show was bad. When all was said and done, TJ and I had three unconnected and disconnected scenes, none of them very compelling. Afterward, we thought about getting an outside eye to help, but we couldn't decide on anyone we were certain shared our same (blurry) vision. We knew we wanted to try to realize this idea of truly committing and reacting honestly in the moment and going wherever that took us. As much as we knew we didn't want to do a show like that first one again, we weren't exactly sure how to get to the next, hopefully, less horrible step.

> *The two took away lessons from that first outing. Most importantly, they realized that dissatisfaction with the current situation was fine. And that, in the future, it would be a better choice to stick in it and try to work their way through it rather than pop away from it. Although the impulse to want to leave a potentially uninteresting scene was real, the reaction of bailing was less than courageous. Even if it took longer than they were comfortable with, they decided that instead of abandoning a scene, they would try to sit in the difficulty, and see what came of it.*

> *TJ felt that the first show seemed to rev them up to try never to be that irrevocably horrible again. And, he felt that one bad show was no reason to stop playing. David was willing to keep showing up, and that was all TJ needed to know. He was willing to keep going onstage with David Pasquesi for as long as he was willing to have him. David was more apprehensive:*

For weeks afterward when TJ and I did the show again, I was often not looking forward to it for fear of messing it up. With our second show, which was thankfully less horrible than the first, TJ and I discovered that another difficulty we wanted to prevent was a prolonged uncertainty about our location. We try to avoid spending a lot of time being confused. When I do shows with other people, a lot of the time I'm unsure of where we are or what is going on, and it prevents me from being present and therefore useful. I don't like fumbling around in the dark, not knowing a single thing, so I decided not to do that anymore onstage. Fortunately, I don't have to with TJ. Either I'm confident that I know what's going on or I don't care that I don't know what's going on. I don't know why that happens with TJ, but it does.

Many of the other components of our show came about by chance during the next couple of performances. For instance, during that second show, we discovered a third character was introduced and needed to be played. Obviously, one of us had to step in and play him. So we did. I had never seen that before, and we had not talked about doing it, but it sure seemed like the next little thing that needed to happen. It worked out pretty well, so we continued playing more characters than there are people in the cast (which, if you're not paying attention, is two). Also, we realized that we seemed to be staying in actual time rather than time dashes (scenes that moved backward or forward in time) like in a Harold. Maybe that was a result of our commitment to play the scene moment by moment. Who knows? That just seemed to be where the show was leading us.

Sticking to real time ended up being a happy accident. It was very helpful in determining the location of subsequent scenes. Since we knew we were in the same time, if a new character appeared with no apparent connection to the scene we had just watched, we realized we must be in a different location.

And if TJ is playing a new character in a different location, he is probably not alone. So I could play someone there with that guy. We still move from scene to scene in this way.

In that second show, we played one long scene, and it was very relaxed, very easy. We found we were attempting something interesting and challenging (at least to us) and something worth trying some more. Eventually, it became apparent we were realizing our original goal: to do the next natural thing and let that moment inform us about what we were already doing.

The structure of our show was being revealed, little by little, as we went along. These were not rules we came up with, nor are they rules we follow. They are just patterns we discovered as we worked together, perhaps because we hadn't set any boundaries, or perhaps just dumb luck. But this show has always wanted to be played in real time. The person who initiates a character has no proprietary rights over that character. We should pay attention to everything the other person does because we may well be called upon to play that character soon.

And we noticed another unspoken element to our show. We learned during the second show that we somehow were able to understand one another's intentions. Either we were both looking very hard and paying very close attention or we had some kind of telepathy. I'm not certain that there is a difference between the two. But I do know it was very strange. I don't have this experience with everyone I improvise with, and I'm not sure TJ does either.

The only other time I've had this connection before was with Joel Murray. But that was understandable. Joel and I knew each other very well. We traveled around to exotic locales together, got in trouble in distant lands, cheated at cards together. After all that, Joel and I can communicate well. But TJ and I hardly knew one another. After the first year of doing shows once a week, I used to say that TJ and I had known one another for exactly fifty-two hours. So it was startling and odd how well we seemed to understand one another from the beginning.

TJ ON MINDREADING

I have felt connected to some other players. I always felt something special with Jack McBrayer, who I've known since our iO and Second City days. But the feeling was different with Dave. I think it's a combination of his calm and focus, the sheer length of the show, and it being just two of us out there together that makes a unique bubble form around the stage. When I'm playing with Dave for that hour, I feel like I've gone away for a while. I can't come back to this world too quickly, or I get the bends. It feels like the bubble seals in a way. It feels quiet and separate from the rest of the world.

> **When I'm playing with Dave for that hour, I feel like I've gone away for a while.**

From the beginning, Dave and I have almost always been of a similar creative mind, even though I am sure I would have gone along with anything he said. We agreed on all the artistic goals for the show. We still try to let the improvisation lead us. Performing together has guided us towards some elements now identified with our show, such as assuming each other's roles, though we're not the only ones who do it. We started doing these things because the show called for them, out of necessity. After that first performance, we were committed to following, rather than guiding, the improvisation. Still, going into that second show I was nervous, but I figured we couldn't be worse than the previous week purely out of the sheer mathematical limits of how bad a show can be.

From show number two up to the present, we've felt that we may be onto something. For us. I'm not saying it's revolutionary in the world of improvisation, but merely that we are onto something that we'd like to explore further. I'm pretty lucky that I get to keep playing with Mr. Pasquesi every week. From my perspective, I have gotten to be around one of the greatest improvisers and dudes who has ever been. Dave excites and educates me. Keeps me honest. Helps me focus.

Since our first show in 2002 until now, Dave and I never agreed to keep going, keep doing shows. We simply agreed to not stop yet. We promised each other that the night we get it right; we quit.

We haven't had to worry about that yet.

PART TWO

DEFINING THE JOB

3

THE JOB OF AN IMPROVISER

> In order to improvise in front of an audience,
> you have to be accepting, involved in the moment, and courageous.
> — *Martin de Maat*

> We are what we repeatedly do.
> Excellence, then, is not an act but a habit.
>
> — *Aristotle*

TJ and David give serious consideration to what they regard as the job of an improviser. The responsibilities do not begin and end on the stage. To them, the job of an improviser is to bring all life experiences to the stage; to approach their time onstage with respect, intelligence, and mindfulness; to have faith in the process; to be trustworthy and to trust in others; and to hone every possible improvisational skill. Above and beyond all else, they say the job of an improviser is to be an exemplary stage partner.

DAVID EXPLAINS

TJ and I believe the job of an improviser is to live an interesting life and share it with your stage partners. The primary duty of an improviser is to be of most use to one's scene partner. In order to do that job, there are certain preparations that help: read; learn to move through fear; pay attention in the world; be an active participant; consciously observe; think. In short, live life mindfully. Be an active observer and an intellectual sponge in relation to the world around you.

Even though we may only see a person for a moment, we can fill in all the unknowable blanks. If I see a young lady in a wheelchair, why isn't she walking? Is it temporary? How is she dealing with it emotionally? Maybe her worry is that others seem to be uncomfortable about it. Maybe she doesn't care what other people think. Or how about a bumpkin in the city with eyes like saucers, an adult looking around like a child in wonder—what is that person like back home? Is he confident and self-assured at work? What role does he play in his family? Our job is to lead a thoughtful and interesting life offstage, outside of the world of improvisation. And then bring all that to our stage partners.

> **The primary duty of an improviser is to be of most use to one's scene partner.**

All that mindfulness cultivated offstage is brought to the stage in service to our scene partners and the show. An improviser needs to read ... and *think*. Our responses and reactions will be, *must be*, colored by our thoughts. So it behooves us to have some.

Overall, I think it is helpful to read, especially books that use a style of speech that communicates efficiently. J.D. Salinger is one of the best examples I know who employs this elegance with his words. His dialogue reveals so much about the characters, relationships, and location without a great deal of backstory. When reading his work, I think, "The only way he would be able to say that to her is if they had a previous experience of ____." For instance, the characters speak the way only siblings would speak—therefore they must be siblings. The exposition is understood without having to be stated.

> *TJ and David both love words, nuances of meaning, turns of phrases, so they naturally bring that to their work. David knows that with TJ's understanding of words, he doesn't choose them by accident. His attention to vocabulary helps David figure out the gravity of a situation, the level of formality between them, the types of people they are. David says if he listens fully, TJ tells him a great deal with his use of language. David's duty is to bring this same thoughtfulness to TJ while TJ views the job differently:*

The job of an improviser is to be as widely talented an improviser as possible. Rather than finding a niche as a type of player, an improviser's responsibility is to seek to do everything well. It's a big job. Though we might be too lazy to memorize a script, being an improviser is not a walk in the park.

An improviser should be able to initiate a scene, make big, structural show moves, edit the scene, do object work, sing the second verse of the song just to buy someone else some time. An improviser should be able to maintain a third eye overhead to recognize what animal is being created onstage and then to ride it. All of it. We should be able to do everything an improviser should be able to do ... and an improviser should be able to do everything.

> **We should be able to do everything an improviser should be able to do ... and an improviser should be able to do everything.**

All these skills are rolled out for the benefit of those onstage with us. Like Dave, I believe an improviser's primary job is to be of most use to our stage partners. In *TJ & Dave*, my job is to figure out how I can be of the greatest service to Dave. I should be identifying things I can do to help the moment, the scene, the show. I should be behaving attentively, with my last thought being about myself. That is my job onstage.

Offstage, an improviser's job is merely to stay alive and pay attention.

We're both huge fans of language. Sometimes it can get the best of us. Sometimes it brings out the best. But always, it's another offering I can bring to the stage to be of better service to David.

Onstage, playing at the top of my intelligence is another way I can bring at least one hundred percent of myself to my partner. When doing a show, there doesn't appear to be a benefit to not being at least as smart as you are. Why would you tie one of your hemispheres behind your back if you don't need to?

> **An improviser's job is merely to stay alive and pay attention.**

Sometimes people think being dumb is funny. Think of a sitcom—there are a lot of dumb people that are funny on TV, so some improvisers may be going for that. Or perhaps some improvisers believe that they'll seem foolish if they make a mistake while trying their best, so it's way more acceptable to make a mistake if they're already acting like an idiot. Maybe playing to the top of your intelligence feels too vulnerable. But do it anyway.

In our show, David is playing at the top of his miles-high intelligence. When we are working together, I trust that David has noticed everything in the scene. So if he chooses not to respond to something immediately, it's still in his pocket. This speaks to trust, but also to the amount of thought that goes into a show. Your brain needs to be firing on all cylinders. You should be using all of your smarts.

> As long as you're doing a show, there doesn't appear to be a benefit to not being at least as smart as you are.

THE STAGE AS A SACRED PLACE

The stage could be thought of as a place better lit than real life, with chairs facing in our direction so people will give us their attention. But it can be more than that. There is that unknown element that brings to the experience something special. In David's opinion, the stage can only take on this extra, perhaps sacred, quality if the performer treats it that way, and the audience will take its cue:

We learned at Second City that wearing a coat and tie informs the audience. It shows them respect and allows them, in turn, to value you. TJ and I dress to convey consideration for the space and the act of improvising, although wearing a suit and tie is not as practical for the performing we do. (We tried it.) Yet, if I walk onstage in shorts and flip-flops, first off, shoot me. Me, an adult in public dressed in shorts and flip-flops? Jesus Christ.

We are only there to help reveal the show. We don't think the audience is there to see us. We think they are there to see what might happen tonight. Our clothing is not to get in the way of the job, which is, of course, first and foremost to be of use to my fellow improviser.

The stage is a sacred space, and to heedlessly take the stage is disrespectful to Improvisation itself. Although developing improvisers should be logging as many hours as possible, an improviser's duty is also to be discriminating, and each time we take the stage should be an effort to improve. My job is to present the very best of myself onstage out of respect for Improvisation itself.

> *TJ thinks folks should play with everybody and at every opportunity. He would say play, play, play! He believes there are benefits from doing every type of show whether he plays a huge 1,500-seat house with David or a small venue with a cast of fifteen.*

TJ EMBRACES VARIETY

I really love not being acquainted with someone's style of play. But I don't think the stage in itself has any sacred properties. It's very special, and what happens there on any given night can be pretty spiritual or uplifting, but a blank stage doesn't have any special significance. It's a workplace and play space and worthy of great respect. The work and play that occurs there deserves respect, and an improviser should approach the stage ready to play. We do what we can to get our minds in the proper place to be a good improviser's partner that night. It's simple. We wouldn't perform stoned or drunk. If a little bit of exercise that day calms us down, we'll try to get some exercise that day. If five minutes of jumping around and screaming gets you into the proper mode to play, do that. But whatever it takes to get there, it's necessary to abandon all baggage before taking the stage. Just leave it outside.

I show respect to the stage and art form by realizing how lucky we are to do the show that night. Not everybody gets to do a show, so improvisers shouldn't forget that we're fortunate. A lot of folks don't get asked to play, and a lot of people who used to play aren't able to anymore. We can display our gratitude by bringing every bit of ourselves to the show. Improvisation is much bigger than any of us, and it can definitely handle everything we've got. We don't know how many shows we get in a lifetime, so there is no excuse not to bring everything we have to each one of them.

4

BEING A GOOD STAGE PARTNER

Finding a compatible partner is no small thing. Improvisers who find someone with complementary strengths, like-minded goals, and a good working relationship are the lucky ones. TJ and David have found that in each other. Like yin and yang, they form a whole greater than the sum of their parts (and their individual improvisational skills are nothing to sneeze at). In *TJ & Dave* shows, they fluidly step in and out of each other's characters, adding dimension and filling out a scene.

In 1989, David won a Chicago Theater Joseph Jefferson Award for his role in the Second City's *The Gods Must be Lazy*. In his acceptance speech, he said, "Our job is to make others look good. By getting this award, I guess I'm not doing my job. I'll try harder next time."

The idea behind being a good stage partner is to put the focus on the other person—the added benefit is taking the onus off of you. You don't have to be funny. You don't have to be brilliant. You just have to be helpful. A fair dose of selflessness is an absolute requirement to being a good improviser. If you believe, as TJ and David do, that your stage partner is the answer to all your problems, then that person is also the answer to how to be a better stage partner.

TJ and David take their responsibility as improvisers seriously to bring their very best to the stage in service to each other, first and foremost.

FINDING WORTHY STAGE PARTNERS

David believes improvisers should initially play with many different types of people and in varied styles at the beginning of their career (if one can call it that) because that's how they expand themselves. It's like the idea of a core curriculum in college. You take classes you never would be drawn to on your own, but they are often the ones you enjoy the most. Improvisers must find people of like mind to improvise with, those interested in the same kind of improvisation. David used to do stand-up as he gained experience, not because he was good at it, but for the stage time and confidence that came from it so he could get better at improvisation. David continues:

The material of my stand-up sets, by the way, tended to be the Roman poet Ovid, Jesus, death, and dick jokes. It's hard to believe I'm not doing stand-up anymore, isn't it? In the beginning, I thought I wanted to be funny, and that making people laugh was the ultimate goal of improvisation. But I learned so much from Del and the people I worked with that my views started to change. I began to find other people interested in the same goals, so I would hang more with them and less with the folks who were doing work that didn't interest me. Gradually, I devoted myself fully to only working with people doing the type of improvisation that appealed most to me: gradually revealed, organic, longform. If I have chosen to be onstage with someone who is after the laugh at any cost, and I think that they are going to patiently discover the wondrous show before us, then I'm an idiot.

Whatever brand of improvisation you prefer, consider your goals in improvisation and find people interested in aiming for that same place. Unlike music or painting, improvisation cannot be done alone. The idea of the group mind—that the whole is greater than the sum of the parts—is only possible if we are working in concert. In a group of six, with three wanting to master shorter, faster, funnier scenes (a noble goal) and three trying to do longer, more genuine, connected scenes (also a noble goal), the likely result will see neither goal achieved. There are people who don't care to do the type of improvisation you're interested in. Forget them. Don't get onstage with them again. They are a waste of your time. I don't believe anyone is going to find a good stage partner by accident. So go find your people, people!

> *TJ says it's not that different from how you pick your friends or how you would be a good friend:*

I try to find people who are kind, fun, and funny, who are interesting, and who show up ready to work, but remember that it's supposed to be a pretty damn good time. I'm sure you can recognize your people: folks who know if you need a little arm around the shoulder or a pat on the fanny. When you walk into a green room and smile when you see them, you've found your people. Most importantly, if you can be that person, then people are going to want to play with you. Be the people you want to play with, people.

There are times we come across people who just can't be reached. If we speak to someone and explain how what they did destroyed the show and they still don't get that, I don't know how to help them. If they can't recognize that their selfish desire for one laugh destroyed something that everyone else built, then I don't think they get anything at all. I agree with David. You are best off without those people.

Dave and I have never had a whiff of trouble with such things. We've both felt challenged as a pair at times. Perhaps we felt the show was becoming stale or uninteresting, and we needed to reinvest and find out why that was happening. But I don't think I've ever felt a challenge between us. It feels like we were both facing some sort of challenge together.

> *TJ and David have never had any bumps in the road as stage partners. If there is a problem in a particular show, they discuss it to figure out where they went astray (usually one of them was not paying close enough attention). Then, they try to see how it can be avoided. A problem can be as simple as one of them looking away, missing key information that was made available. Many problems can be avoided merely by looking at one another. TJ and David don't believe they have those bigger problems because they are after the same thing. They agree on the type of improvisation they want to do together and the importance of being a good stage partner.*

In TJ & Dave *shows, TJ doesn't consciously think of being a good stage partner to David. "He doesn't need much help from me to look good," he says. "And what seems to make us both look all right as a pair is staying singularly focused on the present moment."*

> **If we believe our stage partner is the answer to all our problems, then he is also the answer to the question of how to be a better stage partner.**

TJ AND DAVID ON GOOD STAGE PARTNERSHIP

The most efficient way to be a good stage partner is to stay in the moment and respond honestly to our partner in a genuine way. In actionable terms, it means literally to look at them. We look to each other to know what to do. We behave genuinely, so our stage partner knows who he is to us. We respond honestly to each other. We talk to our partner in a way we would talk to someone who is *exactly him*. There are myriad ways to help our stage partner look good and all of them require us to pay attention.

> **The most efficient way to be a good stage partner is to stay in the moment and respond honestly to our partner in a genuine way.**

When TJ plays with a new or less experienced person, or when someone seems nervous, he gives a more emotionally laden opening, being more specific with his details, to make an easier set. He is slightly more overt about who they might be to each other, like "Oh, Andy, I'm so glad it was you who walked through that door," or, "We're going to have a great time now! Chuck's here!"—something that will ideally be fun with emotional potential.

Being a good stage partner is being a good improviser. We do this by paying attention to how we can be of service. We are dependent upon our scene partners. They're not lucky to be onstage with us; we're lucky to be onstage with them.

> **Being a good stage partner is being a good improviser.**

Even when not in the scene, a good stage partner continues this same attentiveness. David remembers Del suggesting improvisers might want to think of themselves as part of the scene going on, even when they are in the back line. "That we are a piece of the scenery in the scene, a coat hook or something in the room—that's our state of mind. We are in the scene but not being noticed, invested but not drawing focus. Also, if we play with this sense of participatory feeling when we're off to the sides, we will be much more likely to be present for a timely edit or character that is being called for. We don't have to worry about how to enter that scene because mentally we're already in it."

TJ remembers an improviser who was a great example of necessary self-forgetting. "I would watch her with intense joy, especially when she was on the sidelines. Completely engaged in watching the ongoing scene, she would nod or shake her head to rhetorical questions that were being asked in the scene, and she would smile when things were joyful. You can watch people on the side who look at their shoes or try to think of what they're going to do for their next scene or predetermine how they're going to initiate the next scene. When I watched her, it was clear this improviser never had any thought for what she was going to do next. She was just living along with the people in the scene that was going on. And it was beautiful to watch."

Being a good improviser requires faith and trust. We need to trust that we are just fine by ourselves. Trust that as an individual, I am okay, while at the same time recognizing that I am completely dependent upon my stage partner. We need to have faith that if we behave this way, the show has a shot at being pretty darn good ... and trust that Improvisation will take care of us.

5

LISTENING
(No, We Mean Really Listening)

So when you are listening to somebody, completely, attentively,
then you are listening not only to the words, but also to the feeling
of what is being conveyed, to the whole of it, not part of it.
— *Jiddu Krishnamurti*

Great ideas ... come into the world as gently as doves ... if we
listen attentively, we shall hear, amid the uproar ... a faint flutter
of wings, the gentle stirring of life and hope.
— *Albert Camus*

There is listening, and then there is Listening. When you watch *TJ & Dave*, the difference becomes clear. Nothing is wasted. Nothing is missed. Nothing is forgotten. Of course, that's not entirely true. TJ and David say that when they evaluate their shows during their debriefing, the wobbly bits are almost always the result of not paying close enough attention. Even in conversation, when you speak to them, you feel heard. They listen to each word. They are truly listening, not planning a funny story on a related topic. Even TJ attests that it is a remarkable experience to be listened to by David Pasquesi, and it takes some getting used to. Most people are not accustomed to receiving that much focus. Being heard in such a way is quite a gift. (Just don't say anything stupid.) To an even greater degree in their show, TJ and David absorb each other's gestures, expressions, and energy, along with the words. The words are only one piece of the puzzle they must solve in order to discover the scene unfolding between and around them.

While their approach to listening can be difficult to break down, the art of paying attention is essential. Their level of listening involves intense attention and energy. TJ and David utilize this approach because they see it as the path of least resistance, which leads to the most honest scenes. As David says in *Trust Us, This is All Made Up*[1] (a documentary on the duo, filmed at New York's Barrow Street Theatre), "If you pay attention rather than try to make stuff up, everything is already there."

DAVID & TJ ON LISTENING

If it is true that our scene partner is the most important person on the planet —and it is—why wouldn't we pay attention and learn all we can from him or her? Listening is a willingness to learn. We gather information through acute listening with all six of our senses. In *TJ & Dave*, we come onto the stage with nothing, like a newborn comes into the world or a Vegas conventioneer leaves his room on a Thursday morning, crying, naked, covered in feces and blood ... and with nothing.

We don't know anything.

Luckily for us, our stage partners provide all we'll need. And their faces, especially the eyes, are the first place to look. Do their eyes look friendly or suspicious? Are they looking at me with familiarity? What does their body language say? In another show, like a Harold, we find it helpful to come onstage with an emotional point of view or a piece of information inspired by a monologue, opening, or audience suggestion. But in *TJ & Dave*, before the lights go up, we assume nothing and we come onstage tabula rasa (that's Latin for "really dumb"). As soon as those lights rise, we listen and pay attention to our scene partners to learn ... *everything.*

Everything is already there.

TJ tells me everything. The way he looks at me tells me who I am. He tells me who he is by how he is standing, moving, sitting, talking. The way he behaves and what he says in front of me tells me about the nature of our relationship. I'm probably not going to tell my boss I pissed myself last night, so I better know for sure that TJ is not my boss before I say anything.

---

[1] *Trust Us This Is All Made Up*, Dir. Alex Karpovsky. Perf. TJ Jagodowski and David Pasquesi. B-Side Entertainment 2009.

We perform as if everything we need to do the show is already onstage with us, and it's our job to pay attention as it's revealed. Dave shares a simple story:

"In one class I taught, everybody was doing stuff that was unmotivated. I told them to get onstage and not move until they had a reason. Somebody fidgeted. I asked them why they were fidgeting. They couldn't answer, so I told them to stop doing it. Everyone stood there, totally frozen. And the longer they stood there, the more in their heads they got, the more into themselves. (I was a bit of a dick about them not moving at all.) Then one guy walked all the way across the stage to tie someone's shoe because the shoe needed tying. It was lovely. It illustrates that the best reason to do anything is to serve another. That's why one should do anything; because they notice it needs doing. I'm not sure that example helped anyone else in the class, but it helped me."

We're not saying that we exclusively focus on wardrobe or concrete. We're saying the untied shoe exemplifies the need to pay attention to the moment and, from that place, choose an action that serves the scene. We cannot think our way out of a problem. When the problem is over-thinking, the answer is not to do more thinking. The solution rests outside of ourselves. And that's why we listen with all our parts and senses to everything happening onstage.

We constantly need to remind ourselves to listen more closely. David has another story. He was at home meditating on the topic, 'How can I be of use?' His son, about six years old at the time, walked in the room:

"Hey, Dad?"

"Just a minute," I said, thinking, 'How can I be of use?'

"Dad?"

"Yeah, in a minute." I continued to ponder, 'How can I be of use?'

"Dad?" My son tried again.

It took him three times. I wasn't listening. I was busy thinking, unable to see that the answer to my question was tapping me on the shoulder.

> **Pay attention to the moment and, from that place, choose an action that serves the scene.**

David's parable illustrates that whatever the problem, the answer is the person standing there next to us. All information. All solutions. It's not me; it's you. Our scene partner is both door and key to the scene we're discovering together. We don't need to invent anything if our inspiration is standing there looking into our eyes. That's why we're supposed to listen. It's in our own best interest. It's self-serving. We listen to our stage partner because we want to be in a great scene, better than any one we could make up by ourselves. They're going to help us do that.

> **Listening is the willingness to learn.**

We believe the scene is revealing itself to us as soon as the lights go up. It is essential to pay attention so that we can figure out what that scene is. But the scene isn't a moment locked in time that we get to examine forever. It changes immediately because we are both responding to the information we receive. So we listen carefully from the first moment a scene begins because, soon enough, that first moment is long gone, with or without us. We stay in the moving moment. The present. We listen. And we react. In this way, listening also is the willingness to change.

One of the many lessons David learned from Del Close was that a line is not delivered until it is received. How can we be sure it's been received? Looking at the person we're talking to is a good start. It's recognition in our partner's eyes. We listen, receive the message, and are changed by it. When we truly listen, whether it's responding to a look, a gesture, or a line being delivered, we are taking in all that information and being affected by it. This is the heart and soul of improvisation. Meanwhile, we're also aware of the messages we're transmitting to our scene partners. We have to be aware of what our body, our face, and our eyes are saying to them and how it's being received. Assessing others and ourselves is in our minds as the lights go up on a *TJ & Dave* show. We begin to learn *everything*, and we don't stop learning until those lights go down about fifty minutes later.

WHAT ARE WE SPECIFICALLY LISTENING FOR?

We listen with all of our senses. Visually, the lights come up. Immediately, we look at the information we have available right now. We ask ourselves, "In this moment, what do I know?" The answers, of course, are in our stage partner. We notice the eyes, proximity, and body language. We notice the perceived sense of status. We notice if it feels like we're inside or outside. It is a process of elimination.

Michelangelo (di Lodovico Buonarroti Simoni) supposedly said something like, "All I had to do was remove all that was not the David from the stone." That's the way TJ pictures the acute listening process during a show, like carving a statue. (Though we are in no way comparing ourselves to the great artist.) In the show's earliest moments, it's like we're lopping off huge slabs of stone in an evolving elimination of possibilities. TJ gives an example, "Say the lights come up, and I see that David is looking at me kindly. It's likely at that moment that we are not sworn enemies. Instantly, that eliminates tons of other possibilities for the dynamic of this relationship. That's a huge piece of stone removed. The way David sits down suggests he is male. So in that moment right there, 51% of the population is eliminated. That's another big piece of marble. Maybe I find myself at the stove, so we know we're in a kitchen of some sort. Another chunk gone, and we begin to get an idea of the shape of the show we're in." Eventually, as we go deeper into the show, we get down to the finer points of the statue, chiseling out the fingers and toes to reveal the small details of the world we now inhabit.

In *TJ & Dave*, we pay attention carefully in order to keep eliminating possibilities until it appears it was always and only this one thing from the start. With each bit of information taking shape, we discover ourselves together in this narrowest sliver of exactly this thing here. This moment, where we are right now.

How it feels is an important part of the listening equation. As David puts it, "I do not have to be able to point to and prove the existence of this new reality or defend my decision to believe a certain thing. I simply sense that TJ is my elementary school teacher from the way he is standing, how it makes me feel, and most of all, that nothing indicated he was not my elementary school teacher. So we sense a particular relationship, which begins generally. In this case, TJ seems to have higher status. I seem to be in a bit of trouble. I learn this information from paying attention to my posture and how TJ is responding to it. Until proven otherwise, it becomes fact." All this is happening as the lights come up, and we begin to assess the intensity of the relationship between these two people. We call this the Heat, and we'll get back to this topic in a bit.

We listen with all our senses, including our emotional reactions and this sort of sixth sense. We're not saying we see dead people. Well, one of us can see dead people, but we can't tell you which one (because it's TJ). We've learned to listen to and trust our gut. Everyone is capable of sensing intangible information in a room, like when you are the first guest at the party. You can tell by the way the hostess answers the door that she and her husband just had a real humdinger of a fight. These are skills we naturally possess. (This sense is related to the Weight, the feeling of something unspoken going on, and we'll dive more deeply into this topic as well in a while.) Just know for now that these gut-level feelings are what we are listening for, and pay close attention.

That's why we don't discount this intangible feeling between us. In fact, we weigh it more heavily than the facts and plots in a scene. As they say about people, there is Bobby and Jane, and there is something between them. We're talking about the something between us. It is not us—either of us—but it is there nonetheless. TJ half-jokingly says that the magic of *TJ & Dave* is in the ampersand. We feel that anyone can hone this sixth sense by remaining open to it, practicing it, and trusting that little inkling is correct. Even though we have no way of knowing what causes that feeling, we still behave as though it is true and trust we are right. Through experience, we have found that when we listen to and trust that little inkling, the shows tend to work out better. So that's what we do.

That's a lot to listen for, right? The eyes, the face, the body. The proximity. The little hunch in your gut, the faint flutter. It takes work and it can be tiring. We don't do it all day long, but we can do it for an hour at a time. And we try to approach it from a place of ease, an almost passive place where all we need to do is listen intensely.

And can we note that we're more than halfway through a chapter on listening, and we have barely mentioned words at all?

Sometimes improvisers mistakenly think that they have to bluff and blabber to cover up the fact that they don't know what's going on at the top of the scene. But if we can quiet mouth and mind, and turn that energy into noticing our partner and the moment we are in, we have a far better chance of being helpful to the scene and show. So we try to hush up, listen, and pay attention.

To this end, we find it essential to remove obstacles that prevent us from listening to the other person onstage:

- We won't listen if we're afraid.
- We won't listen if we think we know how the scene is going to go.
- We sure as hell won't listen if we're thinking about what funny thing we're going to say or do.
- We won't listen if there are way too many bees in the room.

> **We won't listen if there are way too many bees in the room.**

All these impediments to good listening make sense when we remember it's human nature to want to do those things. The reason we want to pre-plan the scene is fear. We're afraid of not knowing what it is about or that it won't be funny. Maybe the audience won't like us, our scene partner will get more laughs, or we'll get stung by Africanized honey bees. In order to improvise well, we need to remember that those reactions to fear are not helpful.

Of course, this state of intensified Paying Attention involves a tremendous amount of remembering. The way to become a better listener is by listening better. Likewise, the way to becoming better at remembering is also by listening (and remembering better). We find that folks tend to stop listening when they believe they know what's going to happen next—or when they know what they *want* to happen next. If we're truly improvising, we can't imagine how we could know what's going to happen next. (If you know how to do that, then your skills are being totally wasted by improvising. You should go to the race track. Save the world or something. For god's sake, Man, you can see into the future!)

The two of us have developed individual approaches to remembering details in a show. David says you can improve your memory by paying attention to the people you speak with, by caring enough to be concerned with what they are saying, and not merely waiting until you can talk about yourself again. Some of the same principles apply in conversation as they do in a scene. You don't need Ginkgo biloba as much as you need to care about the other person.

TJ helps his memory through specificity and emotional touch points. "I use names that fit personalities to help me remember them. Though it seems like a lot, I find it easier to remember details. I would remember eating pea soup with dill croutons or thinking of buying an 82 Merc, rather than having a 'meal' or buying a 'car.' But most importantly, I try to remember the feel of the scene, the emotion in a relationship. It's more important and useful. Even if, heaven forbid, I forget my wife's name, I will remember the feelings that played between us."

Maybe at this point you're saying, "Oh, man. Look. Listen. Notice. Pay attention. Trust my gut. And now I have to *remember* too? What the hell?" We know it's hard reading a book about these things ... until you get onstage and start doing it. And it's not going to happen by accident—you have to get onstage with people who want to work this way. It's not that tough. You just have to take the next step on the path in front of you. You don't have to invent. You just have to notice. You don't have to play the whole show. You just have to play this moment. Now this moment. *Now this moment.* That is all we're responsible for. We're only responsible for right now. But if we're not listening, we'll miss this moment.

For those who have just joined us, wisely deciding to start reading on this page, we will reward your prescience with some super secret information: **Listening is all there is.** It is the basis for everything we do. (But we'll talk about other stuff too, because we couldn't charge much for a five-word book.)

> **Listening is all there is.**

IN CONVERSATION: *LISTENING IS MORE THAN HEARING WORDS*

> The humble listen to their brothers and sisters because they
> assume they have something to learn. They are open to correction,
> and they become wiser through it.
> — *Thomas Dubay*

> Sometimes I suggest that we perform onstage
> as though we are a whole bunch of raving paranoids ...
> nothing that I hear is going to be simple,
> nothing that you say to me is going to be accepted at face value.
> — *Del Close*

We wrote this book using a long series of conversations, which tended to dive into some arcane detail. These conversation portions delve more deeply into select elements of David and TJ's approach to improvisation. Please order a drink, pull up a chair, and join us.

DAVID: The other night, TJ and I did our show following a nice afternoon discussion with very smart guys [Robert Krulwich and Jad Abumrad on the *Radiolab* podcast] about the mystical aspects of not-knowing and improvisation. It was a fascinating talk. I don't recall being more hack in a long time.

TJ: I have no sense of why you feel that way.

DAVID: That's not to say I haven't been more hack. Just that I don't recall. I suppose I was listening but not being affected by it.

TJ: But if I'm not giving you things that elicit an emotional response, then it's my fault.

DAVID: I guess this goes to the idea of listening ... to listen for the truth. Not just the words. The other week, one of TJ's characters said out of the blue, "I'm not a failure." Now I could have just listened to the words alone; if I had taken that statement on face value, there is no problem. But that isn't what he was saying. TJ was asking for help.

TJ: It's never the words as much as the way you say them. If I'm not emotionally attached to those words, then I'm still giving you blank paper.

PAM: TJ's character is asking for help?

DAVID: Yes, his character. If TJ the guy were asking me for help, he'd say something like, "Hey. I need some help." I would bet that in the middle of a show, TJ could say, "Hey, my ticker's a little off," and I would probably know that he was actually having a heart attack.

PAM: The truth is the emotional attachment?

DAVID: Yes, the *meaning* of the words.

TJ: The truth is almost always behind the words. We almost never are saying what we're saying when we're saying what we're saying.

DAVID: Except in very boring scenes.

PAM: So, in that scene, "I'm not a failure." meant, "I need help not failing"?

DAVID: In that case, I think it meant, "Help me." But he's not going to tell me how to help. He's going to leave that up to me—to help or not.

TJ: A line like, "You look rested" could mean, "I slept like crap, and I resent you right now."

PAM: So words are on one level and the emotional intent on another. You're listening for both.

TJ: You listen to look through the words.

DAVID: When doing the job of an improviser well, one is listening for both. What is truly being communicated?

TJ: Subtext. Whys. Clues and reasons.

DAVID: And the deeper the meaning, the more interesting.

> **You listen to look through the words.**

PAM: Is it cerebral or emotional, this part of the listening?

DAVID: All.

PAM: You're listening for words and emotions. Is there another level of listening? Your approach to listening seems like a Vulcan chessboard.

TJ: There is a factual level that you need to be responsible for. For instance, the fact that Dave is speaking of his aunt's death. But, what's more important is that he speaks like he lost a lover.

DAVID: We are paying attention to the honest feelings and responses in ourselves. Like, "Wow, that makes me sad. Why does his not knowing he's not a failure make me sad?" Then I start to go through some possibilities:

a.) He is always very strong. Wonder what's wrong?

b.) The poor guy doesn't know how great he is.

c.) Oh God ... he finally figured it out ... he is a failure. Now what?

PAM: And then you choose one of those to respond to? So you're responding to how the words made you feel?

DAVID: Or not choose. It isn't choices; I don't think. But, yes, combined with all the other stuff, you're responding to the truth. It is unhelpful to respond to a lie.

PAM: The lie is his words?

DAVID: Yes, in that case.

PAM: You aren't playing slowly; you're playing super fast. You're processing an incredible amount of information in an instant.

DAVID: TJ and I come on knowing nothing. So we need to learn everything.

PAM: I taught a workshop that focused on listening at the top of a scene and someone realized that, onstage, we tend to forget that around ninety percent of communication in life is nonverbal. Onstage we tend to rely on the paltry ten percent provided by words alone.

DAVID: Absolutely. But we're talking about ideals. This insane level of paying attention is the goal. I don't come close to achieving it. It is a Herculean task. But we do know that is the goal.

PAM: You suggested that you two might communicate onstage as TJ and David rather than your characters (such as the heart attack thing, which I dearly hope you never have to test). Do you really do that during shows? Do you listen for that?

DAVID: Not much as TJ Jagodowski and David Pasquesi. Except perhaps moments when we're enjoying doing something we know is absurd for the other guy.

TJ: I assume Dave is always a character. But I hope that if he spoke to me directly, I would know. I did tell that to Dave once in New York, the heart thing, and he knew. But we addressed it internal to the show.

PAM: That actually happened in a show?

TJ: Yeah. I felt heart attack-y.

PAM: Oh no. What happened?

DAVID: He died.

TJ: Felt great since then.

PAM: The heart attack-y feeling passed?

DAVID: Yes. Then he died of a brain aneurysm. No one saw it coming.

TJ: Eventually, it passed. I changed to another character who felt a lot better.

DAVID: And then I had to play his guy. My reaction was very different at having a heart attack ... So peaceful.

6

SHUT UP
(No, We Mean Really Shut Up)

> A dog is not considered a good dog because he is a good barker.
> A man is not considered a good man because he is a good talker.
> — *Buddha*

If you stepped into a typical improvisation show, you could safely bet that you would see two people standing onstage and talking. And talking. Lots of talking. It's understandable. Silence onstage can feel scary. Maybe the audience will lose interest or feel uncomfortable, or another actor will say something funny before you do. When improvisers deliver a constant stream of words, they miss one of the most powerful weapons in their arsenal: Silence. Want to get the audience to lean forward in rapt attention and scoot to the edges of their seats? TJ and David suggest you may want to stop talking for a moment.

TJ AND DAVID ON … SILENCE!

When all goes well, we try to command the words rather than allowing them to command us. As the director and prolific screenwriter Leo Benvenuti once said of a young lady, "She thinks improvisation is talking onstage." But improvisation is not talking onstage. Improvisation is listening. (In case you missed it, listening is all there is.) The more we talk, the less it means. We can simply stop talking and see what happens.

Folks say something and then repeat it in many different ways, saying the same thing again. All wasted. We prefer silence or to speak sparingly and precisely. If our stage partner did not fully understand, *then* we can explain. We always have that wonderful option to respond with silence. Some people believe that the only way to answer a line is with more words, but instead their statement might evoke a silent response. Sometimes we need to think about stuff first. It's not that their line wasn't heard or answered. It was answered, but the answer needed to take the time it deserved to form as it would. And sometimes that involves quiet.

> **You always have the wonderful option to respond with silence.**

Remember, thinking is a perfectly valid response. Say we're doing a scene where we find two kids making brownies together. They are involved in the activity of making those brownies. And suddenly one of them asks, "Are we still best friends?" And the other kid stops what he's doing to think about it. Hmm. Are they still best friends? His silence is far more interesting and useful than a knee-jerk, "Yes."

Sometimes as audience members, we feel less connected to the players onstage when we hear conversations that would never happen in reality. These scenes feel graceless. It's not always the content that makes those scenes feel this way. It's their frantic pace and volume. When improvisers get nervous, an unhelpful internal dialogue can start up. And that can often lead to a plan of action such as, "I'm just going to keep speaking really quickly and loudly until I find something 'good' or 'comical' to say."

We try not to do that.

It's natural to worry that we're not doing "enough" onstage. We spent many years wrestling with this fear. In fact, *TJ & Dave* was created out of a desire to see if we could perform something worth watching through pure moment-by-moment discovery. We wanted to create something from moments of nothing. And we found out that it's impossible to do nothing onstage. Try it sometime. (Then try it some more.) If you're like us, you may find yourself trying to observe what is happening as you're "doing nothing"— which is, in itself, something. And chances are, you'll find yourself with something more interesting than being scared of the quiet and making an easy joke. We're saying this because we have been there. There are times when we speak when we should be listening and when we repeat ourselves. But our aim is to speak mindfully and allow space for silence when warranted.

In *TJ & Dave*, our aim is to represent real life onstage. Silence is often part of real life. Think of recent conversations you have had. Whether important or mundane, it's likely there were pauses—to breathe, to absorb, to sympathize, to stifle an inappropriate laugh—in short, to listen and to react. Think of some of your favorite moments from stage, screen, and life, and many of these moments were often silent or just a small reaction. (Granted there are some readers whose favorite parts of films genuinely are when someone gets kicked in the nuts. To them we say, "This book may not be for you ... But we're sure you'll love our other title, *Nut-Kicking II, Still Kickin' Nuts*.") In any case, if we understand the role of silence in how we communicate in real life, why wouldn't we do this onstage? If this is what we enjoy, why not give the audience a chance to enjoy the same? Lately, we've been challenging ourselves to "Dare to bore." It's our way of remembering that we should never force the show to be funny or comedic, even at the cost of being mundane. Scenes need to move at the speed of life. And sometimes life takes time to reflect quietly.

> **In *TJ & Dave*, our aim is to represent real life onstage.**

When performers load exposition at the top of the show, they assume the audience and/or their stage partner is not on the same page. We'll hear improvisers say something like, "Well, Ron, you and I have been brothers-in-law for ten years ..." But when is the last time you've ever heard something like that in real life? If we went around in our real lives saying, "Greetings, bald guy who married my sister. Haven't seen you since you were kicked out of her house seventeen months ago," we'd end up with a lot of strange looks because that is a crazy way to talk to someone. Unless the person next to you is waking up from a long-term coma or suffering from Alzheimer's, it's insulting to their intelligence to announce who they are to you in real life. Why would we do it in improvisation? When folks get wordy at the top of the scene, those lines are designed to inform the audience, but guess what? The audience already *knows*. And they don't necessarily care. As you'll see in the chapter about Heat and Weight, it doesn't matter that we know the title of this relationship is "brothers-in-law." What counts for us is that we shoulder-chuck each other and throw barbs at each other because we *love* each other. That's what's important about the relationship. And we don't need to talk about it as much as live it.

If an improviser is over-talking, he probably has gotten too focused on plot or the situation. He's become too interested in the facts and too disinterested in the relationship. He's forgotten what's important. Our relationship is the only safe place. When we're feeling lost or stuck in our heads, we look to our partner and notice them. We try to join our partner in the here and now. Voilà. We are out of our heads, not scared. If our stage partner is the answer to all our problems, why not this one too? We are not stand-up comedians. We don't have to gut it out all by ourselves onstage. The cavalry is right there. Our partner is in the present moment, and that's where we need to be if we want to be in the scene with them. Frankly, we don't find that talking helps to figure any of that out. (Listening sure does help though.)

So ... how to get better at this?

Practice.

And now we will take our own advice and shut the hell up.

IN CONVERSATION: *SPEAKING OF SILENCE*

The quieter you become, the more you are able to hear.

– Ram Dass

—————————————

DAVID: Listening is all there is.

PAM: An improviser might ask, "But what am I supposed to say?"

DAVID: Try saying nothing at all. There's a Del story ...

We all were doing monologues. That's how we used to start Harolds. Seven of us, all doing monologues of about two minutes each. Del stops us.

"Those were all not good," he says. We were hurt. He was right, but we were hurt.

Then he said, "No. Do them again. This time you're all poets. Your words are far more important than you think. Use them sparingly. They're powerful." (Or something like that.)

We do our monologues again, all of us were more succinct. And the monologues were so much better. Infinitely. Objectively, markedly better.

End of story.

PAM: You're saying improvisers should speak in haikus.

DAVID: I said "End of story!" I have a tendency to yammer on. Apparently, less is more.

PAM: When I yammer on, it's usually because I'm thinking out loud, casting about, trying to find my way. All the while, my lips are moving and "Blahblahblah" is coming out.

DAVID: I understand. Waiting is also an option.

[Post script: We consider TJ's contribution to the conversation to be the most important insight.]

7

FUCK THE RULES

There are no rules for good photographs, there are only
good photographs.

— *Ansel Adams*

Here's a bit of improvisation history for you. In the late-1950s, "The Kitchen Rules" were created by two pioneers of American improvisation: Elaine May and Theodore J. Flicker. They would gather around the kitchen table, breaking down what worked and what didn't in their previous night's improvised scenarios. These discoveries would fuel subsequent rehearsals with the rest of the members of the St. Louis Compass.

 St. Louis Compass included, at various times, Paul Dooley, Mike Nichols, Elaine May, Theodore J. Flicker, Jo Henderson, Nancy Ponder, Severn Darden, and Del Close.

According to Kim "Howard" Johnson's exceptional Del Close biography, *The Funniest One in the Room*, [Elaine] May began examining the nature of improvisation with Flicker. They examined why it worked, why it failed, and whether there was a way to develop rules that would consistently reduce failure onstage."[1] According to Howard's book, there were three central rules May and Flicker decided on: "Never deny reality ... Take the active choice ... It's the actor's business to justify whatever happens onstage." (Another classic Elaine May tip was, "When in doubt, seduce." This tenet is, in fact, all about making your scene partner the most important person and putting an improviser in a state of emotional connection.)

---

(1) Johnson, Kim H. *The Funniest One in the Room: The Lives and Legends of Del Close.* Chicago, IL: Chicago Review, 2008. 52-53.

Del and some other company members noticed that scenes in which players had conflict and argument were less successful than those in which players agreed with each other. Thus, agreement became a rule of thumb in improvisation. Later, that idea was distilled to "Yes, and ..." now key words of improvisation. Other improvisation pioneers, such as Viola Spolin, Keith Johnstone, and Paul Sills, came up with similar ground rules. Over the years, many of these rules were formalized and more were added. Today's beginning improvisation classes often present a slew of rules.

Now that you know the historical basis of "The Rules," you are invited to forget them. As you will see, TJ and David don't hold much truck in rules.

HERE'S WHAT THEY SAY:

People seem to like rules. There are a lot of rules in our world, governing the way we walk, play games, how we dress, board a plane, and even what we inhale. Improvisation has not escaped the reach of rules. Let's see ... for example, here are some rules often bandied about:

1.) Always say, "Yes, and ...." Never say, "No."

2.) Know one another.

3.) Never ask questions.

4.) Don't talk about the past.

5.) Get out the "who, what, and where" as quickly as possible.

6.) Don't do transaction or teaching scenes.

7.) Show, don't tell.

There are also the aforementioned "Kitchen Rules." We would never, *ever* say those great improvisers were or are anything but great, but we don't believe it was their intent to handcuff future improvisers. Human nature being what it is, we tie ourselves very tightly to word-by-word edicts, which in this case often leads to the mindless devotion to many rules, which often supersede their usefulness.

What people often forget is that so-called rules simply happen to be a collection of observations of characteristics that many good scenes consistently tend to have. But correlation doesn't necessarily imply causation. If you're like us (and if you are like us, have your prostate examined because something is a little off), you may be asking yourself, "Why do these characteristics tend to work?" Well, let's go through that list of seven rules.

Rule number one: Always say, "Yes, and ..." Though agreement (of the established reality) is necessary, we're not keen on parroting the words "Yes, and ..." as it tends to lead to unreasoned acceptance of every offer made. Number two: Know One Another. We are taught that our characters should know each other because scenes seem to work better when we have a common history that could involve an emotional past. It also helps to avoid the small talk of first meetings. Sometimes. (We've certainly done shows where the characters started out as total strangers, and they seemed to turn out equally well or as poorly as shows where the characters know each other.) Number three: Never ask questions. This rule exists because statements are liable to forward the scene and relationship more than questions would. *Some* questions, that is. It's worth noting that the questions folks were trying to avoid were of the "Where are we?" and "What is that?" variety—selfish questions. These selfishly require one's partner to provide all the scene information out of fear of having to shoulder that responsibility.

Questions such as "How have you been since your ma got sick?" can provide information and bring us to an emotional present. That's a good thing—so we don't put much stock in "Don't ask questions" as a blanket rule. Rule four tells us not to talk about the past, because the present is where the scene is happening, and focusing there is most helpful. This rule seeks to avoid a series of purposefully comedic, self-serving, "This one time, in college ... "-type stories, yet sometimes the past bears on the present. Sometimes real human beings tell stories about the past.

As for rule number five's "who, what, and where" ... never mind about that one. Artificially laying those on in the first few lines only gets in the way. They'll reveal themselves if you purely improvise honest scenes. Number six suggests we avoid transactions and teaching scenes because those scenes don't necessarily have any emotional connection, so they are less interesting. But you can do a transaction scene that has emotional connections, or start a teaching scene that becomes something more. And finally, the "Show, don't tell" rule was found to be helpful because choosing action or emotion is far more interesting than just talking about it. That one is true.

As much as these rules make sense in theory, the fact remains that there have been transaction scenes that were entertaining as hell—utterly charming scenes between strangers, and captivating scenes in which the who, the what, and the where are never mentioned explicitly. We're sorry to break it to you, but we could follow all the rules to a T and have very boring or just plain bad scenes (or both). We see it all the time. We do it all the time.

Even though we agree those rules can be helpful, we question blindly clinging to them as necessary for an improviser's mindset. When we hear the argument that these rules are particularly useful for beginning improvisers, we tend to think that they found the rules useful merely because they were exposed to them. We suggest that had they not been exposed to those rules, but some other ideas instead, they would have found that of benefit also. There is perhaps a better (sloppier and scarier) way to learn about improvisation. As much as we want to believe that by following all the rules, we'll end up at the desired destination, the fact is that there were good improvised scenes long before there were rules of improvisation.

When we run workshops, sometimes we do a little experiment. Rather than burden folks with rules, we simply instruct people to behave and respond honestly. That's all. That's the whole enchilada. In the scenes that follow that instruction, sometimes all these rules are broken: People ask questions, strangers have contentious discussions, and there are recollections of the past. And the scenes are often successful and fascinating. If we respond honestly, we don't have to remember any rules. The only thing we need to know in order to improvise is how to make it real. Our only task is to reveal what is already occurring. That's why we *pay attention* to the scene.

> **Behave honestly and respond honestly.**
> **That's all.**

Clearly, we don't think the rules are terribly important. However, we do consider the principles *behind* the rules to be helpful. So chuck the rules, and in their place, try on these underlying fundamentals:

A.) Agree. (This is different than saying yes.)

ii.) Pay Attention.

4.) (or 1A) Don't deny an established reality.

C.) Care for one another.

XII.) The other person is the most important person and the answer to your problems.

12.) Artificially imposing facts on a scene is unhelpful.

n.) The scene lies in the connection between the characters.

12a.) Play at the top of your intelligence (with the understanding that intelligence comes in many forms).

And we would add another one, which so happens to be our central, defining principle. We're going to number it one because it deserves the number one. And it goes like this:

1.) Always behave and respond honestly in the moment.

In order to abide by the number one principle, we have to be right here and right now. We need to know what is happening as well as what has happened or has been established up until this point.

We find when we follow this ultimate principle the scene works out just fine. Isn't that the goal? The goal is not to obey every rule. For us at least, the goal is excellence in improvisation. As far as we can tell, the only way to do that is to **be in the moment**. Now. And now. And now.

We often walk off stage wondering if the show was any good; we never walk off stage concerned that we followed all the rules.

IN CONVERSATION: ON THE PHRASE "YES, AND ..."

"Yes, and ..." is probably the number one rule taught on the first day of every improv class. It is thought to be the cornerstone of improvisation. It speaks to the nature of agreement and refers to the words a player could use when accepting another player's offer and adding to it. "Let's go swimming" could be answered with "Yes, and I'll bring the beer." The premise of the rule is that it's better to agree and forward a scene rather than block someone's offer: "Let's go swimming," is blocked with "Nah, swimming sucks." As the two players negotiate what they're going to do, the audience may become bored, so it's considered bad form. "Yes, and ..." is considered a requirement onstage. Let's dig deeper into TJ and David's belief that "Yes, and ..." are two of the most misunderstood words in improvisation.

DAVID: If you establish a bonfire onstage—and we agree it is a bonfire— and then you tell me to jump into the fire, the *letter* of the "Yes, and ..." law is for me to say, "Yes, I will jump in the fire. And I will dance." But if it really is a fire, the *spirit* of "Yes, and ..." will sound more like "GO FUCK YOURSELF!"

TJ: When we were starting out, we thought we had to use those exact words, "Yes, and ..." What a crap day of scenes that was.

DAVID: We prefer to incorporate the *idea* of "Yes, and ..." as an agreement to the reality of an established scene than actually say the specific words "Yes, and ...." As with a lot of stuff, words are the problem more often than the solution.

TJ: The spirit of "Yes, and ..." as we read it, is an agreement to the present and to deal with it as actual. I don't literally have to agree with everything Dave says or say "Yes" all the time. If he invites me to the beach and my character doesn't like sand, I will say no.

DAVID: NO. GO FUCK YOURSELF.

TJ: Like that.

PAM: You're saying that the idea of "Yes, and ..." is an agreement to the reality established in the scene. The fire in the bonfire scene is the reality, and how you react to that reality is up to you.

DAVID: Well ... it isn't exclusively up to me. I have to react honestly.

TJ: And remain faithful to who you have already been in the scene ...

DAVID: ... which makes it really easy, and less of a choice or a decision plucked out of myriad possibilities. It's just the next thing. The next little thing.

PAM: So if I say "Go jump into the fire," then you say, "Go fuck yourself," how does that avoid the common pitfall of becoming an argument? I think avoiding an argument is one of the reasons "Yes, and ..." is utilized. So show me that scene ...

TJ says, "Go jump into the fire." David says, "Go fuck yourself."

TJ: [Lights! And we never perform again.]

DAVID: "Good night everybody ..." Waving as we exit ... stage left, even. TJ would never tell me to jump in the fire. We would warm ourselves, dry ourselves, relate to one another.

TJ: I don't think I can play that scene. I imagine it as the first line of our show, and if that's the case, then I have clearly lost my mind or decided to make an enemy of the actual David Pasquesi. Either way it's abhorrent.

DAVID: I think part of the problem is that some people think a scene requires drastic actions, like jumping into a fire. In fact, the more interesting scene is two guys drying themselves by the fire, having gotten wet in some way that will be revealed. Some simple thing. The scene is between the two guys, not between them and an action.

PAM: TJ said that "Yes, and ..." leads people to say "a baloney yes instead of a true no." So, saying yes because they think they have to say yes, even if it's not in agreement with the reality established in the scene is a baloney yes.

> **The improviser should respect the spirit of "Yes, and ..."
> but not necessarily the words themselves.**

TJ: We're told to offer these automatic yeses that end up reading like the bullshit they are. Instead, be honest to the point of view that you've found yourself in.

DAVID: I am not responding to the suggestion in a vacuum.

PAM: The "Yes, and ..." is an agreement to the emotion ...

TJ: ... and to the reality of the scene ...

DAVID: ... and to all the things that have come before as well. Even if that line is the first word of a scene, a lot has come before it.

TJ: You agree to the moment you find yourself in, who you are, and what you were. Who your partner is and was. The emotion, the weather, the hour. You name it. The world you have made in that second. All that goes into the moment someone asked you to jump into the fire.

PAM: *Words* may be the least important elements of improvisation.

DAVID: Aha!

8

THE IMPORTANCE OF DISAGREEMENT IN AGREEMENT

No legacy is so rich as honesty.
— *William Shakespeare,*
All's Well that Ends Well

Early in improvisers' careers, they are often taught that they should agree; if one person is excited about something, they must all be excited. This lesson is taught to help move the scenes forward and avoid them turning into senseless arguments. The rule of agreement stands in order to keep people out of each other's way and point them in the same direction. But TJ and David believe that some disagreeing can be a form of agreement:

TJ AND DAVID ON AGREEMENT

Agreement in improvisation is between performers who have contracted to agree to the established reality of a scene. They must always agree to what's real, even while characters may disagree on how they feel about that reality. Occasionally, our characters will have an honest argument in a scene. And we're okay with that. It's fine to disagree if we actually do and can support our contrasting views. The "Don't argue" rule can be unhelpful and misleading, and many times, interesting ideas come from differing points of view.

> **Improvisers must always be in agreement;**
> **characters may disagree.**

One time we did an entire show around a disagreement between a guy who was trying to get into a club and the bouncer who refused him entry. The guy really wanted to go in and dance. The bouncer said, and truly believed, the club was at capacity. Half an hour passed with both characters doing a "Let me in the door" / "No, you can't get in the door" dance, with one character trying to fulfill his want and the other doing his job as best he could. The scene developed into a conversation about belonging and needing to feel a change in one's life, trying new things and finding one's wings at a later stage. Neither player could satisfy the other's desire. The guy wanting to dance couldn't just go away, and the bouncer could not give him entry merely to obey the rule of "Yes, and ..." Finally, someone walked out of the club, giving the bouncer sufficient reason to change his stance and let the man enter.

Disagreement between those characters exemplifies agreement to the truth created in the scene. Despite their argument, there was an agreement to the reality in the scene, the true spirit of "Yes, and ..." If we had followed the misunderstood letter of the "Yes, and ..." law, the bouncer would have let the other guy in immediately. That's a very different scene. In fact, it would have defied the truths that had been felt and postponed any meaningful interaction, just pushing it down the line. But the scene was already there, the conflict was not contrived. We were not arguing for argument's sake. The characters behaved in accordance with what was established.

Let's be clear. Differences of opinion about *actual ideas* will not harm the scene. Still, we're not encouraging argument about menial things, like whether a car is a Honda Civic or an Accord, which might just be a frightened improviser's way to avoid taking action. But if we're dealing with real meaty scenes in which disagreement is the most honest response our characters can make, stating our point of view can be valuable in maintaining the reality of the scene.

Meaningful debate can be a form of respect to our partner and the ideas at hand, assuring each other that we are actually listening and not glibly passing over the important thing going on right under our noses just for the sake of a blanket "Yes, and ...." We need not listen if we know our response will be "Yes." Tussling a little in a scene shows that we care about our scene partners and their thoughts. An honest disagreement where we are invested in a point of view? That sounds like it might be interesting.

9

BEING FUNNY ISN'T THE GOAL

There's a hell of a difference between wisecracking and wit.
Wit has truth in it; wisecracking is simply calisthenics with words.
— *Dorothy Parker*

If you tell truth you don't have to remember anything.
— *Mark Twain*

Of longform, Del Close reflected, "Is what we're doing comedy? Probably not. Is it funny? Probably yes."[1] TJ realized that, in improvisation, being clever could be used as an insult. TJ and David do not claim they perform improvisational comedy, only improvisation. They strive to be honest rather than funny.

Getting laughs is not a goal for everyone. TJ and David's admittedly unattainable goal is to have a perfect show. To that end, they believe honesty, not comedy, is the most direct path. The irony is, their search for honesty rather than laughs often creates funny moments in a *TJ & Dave* show.

You may think, "Hey! Don't they advertise their show as comedy? Don't they promise the audience laughter?" They do not. Improvisation serves all kinds of honorable comedic pursuits, including charades, games, shortform scenes, montages, and Harolds, all of which maintain different relationships with laughter. But in their show together, TJ and David are trying to approach excellence with longform, two-person, intertwined, improvised scenes. Exclusively.

---

(1) Halpern, Charna, Del Close, and Kim H. Johnson. *Truth in Comedy: The Manual of Improvisation.* Colorado Springs: Meriwether Pub., 1994.

TJ AND DAVID ON THE GOAL

When asked how to be funny in improvisation, we answer, "Be honest." When asked how to be honest, we answer, "Just be." To us, improvisation does not mean being funny. It means being human—or better yet, just being.

> **To us, improvisation does not mean being funny. It means being human—or better yet, just being.**

Finding honesty is a deceptively simple endeavor that involves as much not doing (not panicking, not bluffing, not doubting) as doing (being present, listening, paying attention). Sometimes during a show, we'll hear laughter and be certain the other guy was doing something, only to learn the audience was laughing at something we did that was genuine and real. Since laughter can be a response to being surprised, what better way to surprise an audience than with honesty? They never see that coming. So why aren't improvisers always genuine onstage? Fear in any form is the obstacle to honesty and, thus, to good improvisation. Some improvisers fear that an honest reaction won't be enough or fear that they're not getting any laughs (while others are). When we tackle the fear, we can take a step closer to behaving honestly. As James Cagney said on acting, "You walk in, plant yourself squarely on both feet, look the other fella in the eye and tell the truth."[2]

> **Instead of playing to the audience's reactions, we find it more useful to develop our comedic conscience, deciding for ourselves what is important.**

We don't waste time contemplating how to amuse an audience. The audience laughs at agreement and specificity. They laugh at surprise. They'll laugh at cheap shots, like negating your scene partner, but that destroys the integrity of a scene. Instead of trying to play to the audience's reactions, we find it more useful to develop our comedic conscience, deciding for ourselves what is important. It's easy to lose your way without an internal compass. Decide what is important to you as an improviser and set your sights on that personal goal. If you are chasing laughs, a.) You're not truly interested in this type of improvisation, and b.) You may well be undermining the scene and your scene partners. Take a moment to decide where you place the most value.

---

(2) Warren, Doug, and James Cagney. *James Cagney: The Authorized Biography.* New York: St. Martin's, 1983. 203.

There is a famous story from the early days of Second City about a scene featuring Del Close and Joan Rivers in which her character tells his character that she wants a divorce.

Del replies, "But, honey, what about the children?"

Joan Rivers snaps back, "We don't have any children."

The audience laughed. But Joan Rivers denied the established reality in the scene. She sold out her partner for a laugh and probably destroyed the trust between them. But she got her laugh, which was her goal. (Good for her? Perhaps. Good for the scene? Not so much.)

If the audience will laugh at a scene-killing joke, why consider laughter part of the equation at all? Concerning ourselves with audience laughter is only important if laughter is the goal. We hope the audience has a good time at our show, but we don't consider their laughter when evaluating the success of a show. In fact, with some of our very favorite *TJ & Dave* scenes, the laughs were nearly non-existent. For us, a captivating silence is as good as, if not better than, a laugh. Comedy is a mere byproduct of our approach to improvisation, and a byproduct is not pursuable. Seeking laughter in improvisation is a fool's errand. Shoot for something more magnificent.

> **Seeking laughter in improvisation is a fool's errand.**

There is a white whale out there in the vast ocean of our imagination called The Great Show. The Great Show is perfection. We know full well that perfection is an unattainable goal, but that's where we're aiming. We know in each show, we won't get there in at least one of a variety of ways. (Don't get ticked at us if the show stinks: Consider yourself warned.) We inevitably will fall short. That is the nature of being mortal. But just because we will never get there doesn't mean it matters less. Sailors don't think they are going to reach the North Star, or even get closer to it, but it's still an excellent point of reference, something toward which to aim.

If we aim for Great and miss, we may still hit some worthy goals: Interesting, Insightful, Challenging, and maybe even Funny. But if we aim for Funny and come up short (which we will ... *always*), there are bad adjectives beneath it: Crummy, Uninteresting, Pathetic, Feeble, Wretched, Desperate and of course, plain old Unfunny. All we can do is hone the skills that might allow for a Great show to happen, like paying attention, listening and staying in the moment.

In our opinion, a Great, and even great, show does more than make you laugh. It sounds corny, but a great show makes you feel something. We could stand there trying to be funny, but that leads to jokey bits and little more. After shows that made people laugh, we felt awful because that's all it did. When we start to improvise with integrity and honesty, gratuitous nonsense doesn't fit in—which is fine, because that won't get us to a great show.

So if the focus is not on funny, where do we put our energy? It's helpful to cultivate a sense of calm readiness, openness, and presence in order to discover the scene we're in. We try to get the hell out of our own way and not clutter up the scene with the so-called "terrific ideas" that we invent. Most of all, we attempt to stay in the moment with our partner. That's where we put our energy. We wish we could offer you some secret formula for getting closer to The Great Show. If we had one, we would have used it by now.

The concern for whether an audience is enjoying itself sometimes makes an improviser play to that laughter because we can put chuckles, cackles, and guffaws on the scale and measure them. If only humans could make a sound as detectable as laughter when we found something interesting, then perhaps those improvisers wouldn't gauge the success of performances on the amount of laughter they heard. It's a shame that other emotions do not produce such immediately perceived responses as laughter. A sound for challenged or interested or absorbed would be much more helpful to us.

> **When performing improvisation, laughter is best left out of the pursuit.**

Not chasing laughter in improvisation is an ideal, but we don't perform in a vacuum. We perform in front of an audience. We perform *for* an audience. We get it. It's difficult not to want more when they're laughing. It's also difficult when they're staring at you silently, and you're doing something you think is compelling. It can throw you. It throws us. We cannot claim that the audience does not affect us. They do. Hopefully, positively. Their encouragement, attentiveness, and interest register on our radars. At best, the audience buoys us. Although we don't consciously seek to please them, the audience's response certainly is in our consciousness. How could it not be? We stand in a room with them, breathing the same air, smelling the same PBR-enhanced smells, hearing the same whirring of soda machines and clinking of glasses. We know that, because we are listening. We hear the audience, but we do our best not to take direction from them. The audience is not in the scene we are trying to discover.

The audience is not in the scene we are trying to discover.

We're also not saying we don't play and have fun with each other during our shows. It's supposed to be a pretty good time. And if it tickles us, we don't shy away from it, in the same way that we don't shy away from something that makes us uncomfortable. If something is fun and it seems to be where the show is going, we'll start playing a little once it feels like the show is capable of flight. For example, in *Trust Us, This is All Made Up*, we have fun in the scene in a bar when we riff on the phrase "covering our bases." About thirty minutes into the show, we were in a bar talking about our softball team being a player short, David found himself saying, "We're trying to cover our bases. Literally." Then mused, "I don't think I've ever actually been able to say that and mean it. We're *literally* covering our bases because we're talking about a softball team ...." We like words and turns of phrase, so that got us going a bit:

TJ: The only other time we could also use it is, say, what if we were chemists, and we had to keep lids on all of everything?

DAVID: Or we tented military properties.

TJ: Yeah, if like we were Christo.

DAVID: Yeah, we'd literally have to cover all our bases.

TJ: I know! If we were a band that just played rhythm section and we were playing outdoors when it was raining, quickly we'd have to ...

TOGETHER: ... yeah, cover all our bases.

TJ: It comes up more often than you'd think.

We were enjoying ourselves at that moment, and when we look back at it, we can see that the audience seemed to be responding too. But that bit of wisecracking took place well into the show. Usually, we won't take a fanciful tangent like that until the work of establishing a solid, real scene is done. If we didn't have something grounded going on at the top of a scene and we started doing a run of silliness, it would be hard to get the show going. It's nearly impossible to build on a base of flimsy levity and sustain it for an hour. It's easier to save the playtime for later, once we've got our footing.

We are shooting for the stars when we get onstage. To us, the goal of improvisation is something that is certainly beyond our reach. So we will fail ... hopefully in a fashion more daring, more bare, more brazen than we've ever failed before.

IN CONVERSATION: *LAUGHTER AND HONESTY AND GREATNESS*

> The greater danger for most of us lies not in setting our aim
> too high and falling short; but in setting our aim too low
> and achieving our mark.
>
> *— Michelangelo*

PAM: Is Great what you're aiming for? Or are you aiming for Brilliant?

DAVID: Above that.

TJ: Our goal each time is to do the best show ever. It's hard to imagine that show being dishonest.

PAM: For me, the Best Show Ever means my partner and I were in the zone throughout the show. Total group mind. Effortless. It has nothing to do with the audience's experience other than they contribute a necessary energy.

DAVID: For me, in the Best Show Ever, no one makes it out alive. Everybody is engulfed by flames.

PAM: I hope I only see that show by video.

DAVID: Coward.

PAM: What do you consider to be the role of humor in comedic improvisation?

TJ: Humor is an ideal byproduct of a good show.

PAM: It's been called a side effect.

TJ: I like byproduct more now. It sounds more sausage-y.

DAVID: Real Upton Sinclair.

TJ: All things being equal if there's a funny way to say something and a not funny way, I'll pick the funny one. But also the re-creation of reality seems to make people laugh, so being honest is a humorous way to go. Our concern is to be faithful to moments.

DAVID: We are honestly not trying to be funny. We don't think about what would be funny. We think about what is the next thing to do which would be the most useful and interesting. Honesty is being true to this moment and all previous moments.

PAM: This idea of honesty feels like trying to gather steam in my hands. I can't quite fully grasp it.

DAVID: We are talking about a kind of integrity. Newer improvisers may well be honest when they do every scene about "I'm scared out of my mind!" That's not what we mean. We mean being true to the scene, being true to what we have already agreed to, and that everything we have agreed to is real.

There are many reasons why this is necessary. If we change the reality, we can't expect anyone to invest in it. For example, walking through a table in a scene. When someone walks through an established table, the reaction is one of universal disappointment. We all feel let down and betrayed: the other improvisers, the audience, everyone. We invested in that reality, and the person who walked through the table betrayed our trust. They wasted our time. Screw them.

TJ: Agreed. The covenant is broken.

DAVID: And the table example is just object work eliciting that response. But it's the same thing when other established truths have been contradicted: "Wait, that guy used to hate that girl, but now, for no reason, he's real nice to her."

PAM: So aiming for honesty, staying in the moment, and being present exclusively to what is being revealed onstage is your best method of achieving The Best Show Ever?

DAVID: It's heading that way. All that stuff is the most effective way to avoid shitting the bed.

TJ: Everything is x factors. All is unknown. The stage is fraught with possibilities for failing. Paying attention and staying momentary is the best way to avoid failure. Shooting for laughs and audience appeal will make you fall into one of those pits.

DAVID: ... a very deep pit, from which you'll have to escape without the help of your scene partner, who you just sold out.

PAM: How can an improviser recognize an honest response as opposed to a knee-jerk, jokey reaction?

TJ: They already know. Everyone does. They just believe that the stage requires something more or different than what they already are and what they already think.

DAVID: It comes down to trust that all will be well if I do the next tiny, seemingly mundane thing.

TJ: It helps if a person is interesting to begin with, as Del says with his quote about an improviser's job is to lead an interesting life. Although I interpret the end of the sentence to be "... and bring it to your partner." Would you agree, Dave?

DAVID: Yes.

PAM: Some players can't see the difference between making improvisational comedy and making a joke. They want to be good players but don't understand how making a joke harms the show. They think the way to art is through jokes.

TJ: They should do stand-up.

DAVID: This type of improvisation isn't for everyone. I did a lot of stand-up, especially in the beginning. It was my paying job while I was doing improvisation, but I know there is a difference between stand-up and improvisation. I choose to do this, though I admire stand-up.

TJ: Trying to pull laughs is the height of selfishness in our art form. We chose a thing built on sharing. If you don't want to do that, do something else.

DAVID: Right. The requirements are different. They HAVE to get laughs in stand-up. We improvisers don't. We HAVE to be honest and consistent.

PAM: As I improved in this form of improvisation, I started to get a stabbing feeling whenever I said something jokey that wasn't true to the scene. The audience laughed. But I died a little inside.

DAVID: Good. That part needs to die.

TJ: Your improvisational conscience develops over time.

DAVID: That's the kind of stuff Del would string you up for so long ago. It helped. It was an artificial motivation at first, "Boy, I don't want Del yelling at me or yelling at me again." After a bit, you see why all on your own.

TJ: Del would make fun of you in front of your classmates. The best in the biz just pulled your pants down. It was strong incentive to get better.

DAVID: Yes, but everybody was in the same boat. It was not gentle, but it was not terrible. And it wasn't just that you didn't want to get yelled at. It was understood that the goal was to make you better. He encouraged good work too.

TJ: It's that feeling of not being able to look at my scene partner in the green room, realizing the audience left, and I might be with this person for years.

PAM: Great point. During a show, how does the audience's laughter affect your performance, if at all?

DAVID: I'd be lying if I said it had no effect on me.

TJ: I really try to ignore it.

DAVID: It comes as an encouragement to keep going. They're saying, "We're with you."

TJ: An audience's laughter fuels me, but I don't let it inform me. It's a very selfish relationship. I take their energy but not their direction. They lift me, but I still do what I want to do.

PAM: Are there instances when an improviser would be wise to ignore the audience's laughter?

TJ: Always.

DAVID: Even though we don't pander or allow them to direct us, they influence us positively. We sure do better shows for a great house than for a hostile group. It factors in. To pretend they aren't there is not the right thing to do, I think ... to not care is closer.

This reminds me of what we say about words. They're there for us to use, not the other way around. The audience and all of their responses (not just laughter) are information. And often I am wrong about what the audience means by their reaction. If the goal lies in the audience, they determine what I should be doing. So if I hear silence, I may want to play broader or less honest because I am sure they just didn't "get it."

PAM: But they may be quiet because they're feeling something.

DAVID: Yes.

PAM: That's a better outcome, right?

DAVID: It's not bad. If I think they're quiet because I lost them, but they're actually completely with us, I will adjust to something false ... And THAT will lose them. In the end, it's none of my business what the audience is doing.

10

ABOUT FEAR

> The brave man is not he who does not feel afraid,
> but he who conquers that fear.
> — *Nelson Mandela*

> The cave you fear to enter holds the treasure you seek.
> — *Joseph Campbell*

Fear-based moves onstage are to blame for most of the missteps an improviser makes. Fear and the panic of stepping into the unknown breed inaction, mindless jokes, and tedium. Fear is an enemy, but it's also a friend.

Not only are improvisers better served by not succumbing to their fears, but also by actively pursuing them, tackling the seemingly scary topics, and making bold, committed moves. More often than not, such brave efforts create great theater. The whole point of improvisation is to go out there with nothing but one's wits and whatever confidence they can summon. Fear is an understandable human reaction to the attempt to fulfill one's part of the contract with the audience. Improvisers hold up their end of that bargain by following what may be a less comfortable path, walking onstage without a plan. As a result, there is this interesting relationship with fear, as it is a route to all improvisational evils, while at the same time marking the way to improvisational good.

TJ and David try to exemplify Del Close's "follow the fear" principle. They aim to follow the truth of the scene, even if it means breaching uncomfortable waters. They ignore the fear of not entertaining the audience and the doubts about their own abilities in order to dedicate themselves to the frightening prospect of not knowing where the scene will lead. They respond moment by moment to what is unfolding, no matter where it seems to go, even if it's well beyond their comfort zones ... or nowhere at all.

TJ AND DAVID ON FEAR

Before shows, we can hear people being seated in the theater. We hear their chatter. We understand they have paid to be entertained by us for an hour or so. And we are well aware we are about to walk onstage with nothing more tangible than three empty chairs to greet us. Do we feel fear? Sure, sometimes. Okay, maybe a lot.

Like most of you, we are human and thus not immune to the evil nagging of doubt and worry. (We even admit to some pre-show gastrointestinal distress.) We all come to the show with our fears, responsibilities, and self-imposed pressures. But an improviser does well to leave that baggage offstage. Finding honesty is what much of this book is about. It seems pretty easy. (It's not.) The search for honesty requires us to quell the fight-or-flight response constantly threatening to put the kibosh on many good onstage moments. Instead of fight or flight, we suggest that you do neither. Neither battle nor bolt from the fear, but rather pay attention and see where it leads. Problems arise when we forget to pay attention, look at our stage partner, or listen with our whole selves. In short, we forget to just do the next little thing. And the major reason we forget is fear. Fear is the away team. Fear is the bad guy in this show. More specifically, succumbing to the fear, which causes us to react without integrity and grace, is the evil archenemy of good improvisation.

It's natural to be nervous when taking the stage, but the audience doesn't want to see it; they will feel uncomfortable for the improviser, who will sense their discomfort. An unpleasant cycle of awkwardness ensues. One way the audience picks up on that discomfort is when a player is chattering on and on. Unlike radio, we don't need to avoid "dead air" as long as someone is doing something. And that something includes listening. Or thinking. Or reacting. A good way to sidestep the fear is to be quiet and listen.

> **Succumbing to the fear, which causes us to react without integrity and grace, is the true archenemy of good improvisation.**

As we'll detail further down, we approach the show one small step at a time, moment to moment, just doing the next little thing. Some improvisers are afraid to do the next little thing because they're fearful about what will happen after that. (Spoiler alert: After that, you do the next little thing again.) Or they worry that the next little thing won't be enough. (It will.) Have you ever watched a scene when you know someone is about to get dumped, but the actor doesn't do it? Because she's afraid the scene would end, she keeps hemming and hawing for five minutes? Go ahead! Dump him. Something always happens after that.

When in life do you think, "Oh my gosh. We shouldn't do this because everything will end"? There's always going to be something happening after that. Even if you die, something will follow. (Like grief. And perhaps that much-ballyhooed white light. And, for sure, decomposition.) Go ahead and take the next step because it's awful to stall out an audience that is already waiting at a finish line while an improviser meanders towards it. We never know where a scene is going to end. Until it does, there will always be something else to do.

Even when we're able to dodge the trepidation of stepping into the unknown, we share the fear that what we're doing is not enough. That one really gets to us. Our task is not to panic when that thought arises. That thought is a lie. If we focus on each other and pay attention in a fully conscious way to serving each moment that presents itself, we leave no opening for the internal dialogue of self-doubt. There is too much going on and something too important happening for there to be space for anything else.

> **"Follow the fear" does not suggest anything about not being afraid. It requires it.**

Like in any worthwhile story, the bad guy is not all bad. There is a good side to fear, though self-doubting fear is to be avoided. "Follow the fear" means to follow the most interesting path, which also may be the most untraveled and uncomfortable. It's scary because we might not have anything interesting or smart or funny to say. We're afraid, but we do it. "Follow the fear" does not suggest anything about not being afraid. It requires it. It requires that we go toward the things that we ordinarily would avoid: difficult moments, challenging characters, unpopular but honest responses. Beyond that, exploring topics such as kindness and empathy may involve traveling into fearful, vulnerable places. In real life, we may guard ourselves with less-than-true responses. We can afford to be honest onstage. Afford to be afraid. Unlikable. Open-hearted, sweet, or tender.

"Follow the fear" can be a guidepost pointing us toward a nice, meaty, sustainable scene. Let's say a couple is about to go out to dinner, and it's become clear throughout the course of the show that this marriage is truly in trouble. What looks like the easier, less frightening route is to engage in a discussion about where to eat, or whether to have Italian, Indian or Chinese. Or maybe they should they order in? The more frightening choice would be to bring up their marriage problems: Should they divorce? Do they need to separate for a while? Do they still love each other at all? In improvisation, we may want to choose the big, difficult questions, the ones that we turn ourselves inside out to avoid in real life.

Ironically, when we engage in these apparently difficult topics, we make our jobs much easier. The heart-to-heart about a failing marriage probably will end up being much more engaging, worthwhile, and sustainable than talking about how good or bad their ricotta filling is in the manicotti. We might not be able to do fifty minutes onstage about pasta, but fifty minutes about a failing marriage? Hell, yeah. Our jobs get a lot easier, because we have more places to go, more things to feel, more situations and relationships to explore.

But we've probably done more shows in which we discussed ricotta filling than shows in which we discussed grand topics like marriage, birth, or death. But it's not about the ricotta. We could do fifty minutes of talking about manicotti but really communicating about a marriage on the skids. So let's be clear that we're not saying we only do scenes about emotionally charged topics. We're saying that if these moments present themselves, we won't shy away. Quite often, when following the moments that make us a bit uneasy, whether because the topics seemed difficult or dull, we find we land in shows that have more room to develop and grow. Things that present themselves as fears (presumably to be avoided at all cost) are actually the opposite. They are fears to be explored at all cost.

Difficult topics may seem scary, but it's usually not their subject matter that makes us nervous onstage, but rather, our concern about our ability to perform it. We did a show once where we found ourselves in the kitchen of a man whose wife had just passed away the week before. And, sure, there may have been a moment at the top of the show when we asked ourselves if we're ready to go in that direction or if we have any good reason not to. But that's where the show was going—that character's wife had clearly died recently. We could only fuck up the show by putting the brakes on or trying to steer it in a different direction. The plot is not frightening in such a show. What makes us nervous is the doubt that we could be good enough actors to pull it off. That's a big one for us: the palpable, internal fear we bring to a show is whether we can portray an emotional state responsibly.

> **The spirit of "Follow the fear" commands us to follow the show.**

We sometimes get nervous about our ability to handle a character previously mentioned in the show. For example, say we've introduced Chuck. He's a badass. He knows how to cut everyone down. He's the president of the company. The man has no weakness and his guns are always loaded. Can we responsibly play that guy? Or, say that we've set up a woman who is so magical, so gorgeous, and so lovely that men literally fall at her feet when she walks down the street. Can we accurately play this person? That's the scary part for us. Wherever the show is going, we have to go too. Who cares if we can't do it well? We have to do it anyway. That's our job.

Maybe fear isn't the thing we're supposed to follow, but the *idea* of the thing we're supposed to follow. As with "Yes, and ..." in which we differentiate the letter of the law from the spirit of the law. We do the same with "Follow the fear." "Follow the fear," in spirit, means don't be afraid to follow the show. This is the show, like it or not. If it turns out that Chuck is a badass, then that's the show. We need to try not to be afraid of what's already there. There is no exit strategy in improvisation. If you're thinking "Aw, man. I'm afraid of that," tough luck. You bought the ticket to the ride without knowing what the ride was going to be. And if it turns out that this moment is what the ride entails, it's too bad if you're afraid, because it's no longer your choice not to do it. Your only choices are either A) to do the show as it is or B) to fuck it up.

Follow the truth. Follow the show, wherever it goes. It doesn't mean we manufacture scary moments on stage—*Vampires! Leeches! Preschoolers!* — or that we must heighten them—*More vampires! More leeches! More preschoolers!* It simply means we don't shy away from them if they reveal themselves. Just as we don't manufacture the show, we don't manufacture fear. We don't want to artificially do *anything*. So, if a serial killer ends up in this show, someone has to suck it up and play him. We can feel like, "Oh, shit. We have to play a serial killer" or "Oh, shit. We get to play a serial killer. Hot diggety!" The fear is there. We neither invent it nor avoid it. Instead, we try to notice it. If the fear is there, pay attention to it. Pay attention to *everything*.

IN CONVERSATION: *FEAR*

There are times when fear is good.
It must keep its watchful place at the heart's controls.
— Aeschylus

Do one thing everyday that scares you.
— Eleanor Roosevelt

_____

Fear is a very personal experience. Most of the time, you can't just will yourself to stop being afraid or think your way out of it. In this conversation, TJ and David open up about their personal experiences with fear.

PAM: It surprises me that you get nervous before a show. I couldn't imagine improvisers of your abilities would have any doubts. What do you do with that feeling? Do you just sit with it? Are you used to it?

DAVID: Hopefully, it will influence everything I do ... *negatively*. But honestly, for me, it is an indication that something is important, that I care, and it's worth getting nervous over. I try to notice the nervousness. That's all. As with the audience, to pretend it's not there is unhelpful to me. It's there, but I'm not going to be driven by it. To fight it is to give it importance.

PAM: What do you do about it?

DAVID: I go jerk off, and then I'm pretty good.

PAM: I suspect that's not an unusual reaction to nerves.

DAVID: To be fair, it's not specific to fear. That's my reaction to anything, both uncomfortable and comfortable.

TJ: A good meal ...

PAM: The sun rising ...

TJ: Fear physically tenses me. Sometimes I tremble. It makes my head cluttered or slow. I try to step away from it somehow, by trying to stretch it out sometimes. I'll loosen my body, and the fear loosens. And I'll remind myself what I'm there to do, which is to listen and pay attention to Dave.

The fears are self-centered, so if I can remind myself of something outside of me that I'm supposed to do, sometimes I can step away from it.

And if all else fails, I just wait for the show to start and hope that the actual act of improvising makes it go away.

DAVID: I actually enjoy that feeling. Rather than trying to get rid of the thrill and excitement, I have to slow it down. Both of us have an equal and opposite reaction to that fear. Neither the fear nor what it does to us are helpful to us.

TJ: In a way, it slows me in the wrong direction and speeds me in the wrong direction. If you let it get to you, fear will stop the correct slow thoughts you're supposed to have and have you going very quickly with thoughts in the wrong direction.

PAM: Fear can slow the intellectual connections and meaningful thoughts. But players overcome with that speeded-up feeling of fear can make desperate choices because their minds are going quickly, and they feel like they have to *do* something. Anything.

DAVID: And the way I think of it is that we don't have to *do* anything. We have to be something. We have to be this person. I can't be no one. So those fears are ridiculous.

PAM: So on any given Wednesday night at 10:15 you're still feeling afraid?

DAVID: Every show.

TJ: Yeah.

PAM: Some shows more than others?

DAVID: New places, new environments.

PAM: When certain people are in the audience, does that bother you?

DAVID: Only family. Other than that, no.

TJ: Mostly the people I care about or really good improvisers, someone whose opinion I really respect and don't want to let down.

DAVID: For me, it's not people I care about necessarily, but people who can negatively affect me later. People who know where the buttons are, like my kids. Those little fuckers.

TJ: I get most nervous about Facebook friends being there.

PAM: How about fear of disappointing each other? Does that figure into it?

TJ: Very much. David is probably the absolute intersection of both of those things, someone I care about and someone whose opinion I respect the most highly.

DAVID: Me too, TJ. But I think we've been doing it so long that ... *[laughs]* ... boy, I've messed this up already with you. I've done terrible things onstage ... and we're still doing it together. These fears are certainly unfounded.

PAM: Can you imagine TJ making a move onstage that would so disappoint you that you wouldn't want to work with him again?

DAVID: I imagine it all the time. *[Laughs.]* And he always disappoints.

PAM: Every time you get onstage, you hope this is going to be the one, the time he disappoints you?

DAVID: And I know exactly how it's going to happen ... he's going to be a raccoon ...

TJ: ... and he tries to make me a raccoon all the time. He says, "Don't you want to wash your meal in the river?"

DAVID: "It's real dark around your eyes ..."

TJ: "I just found you digging around in those garbage cans by the motion sensor lights ..."

DAVID: "... don't worry, I won't corner you."

PAM: And yet here you are.

DAVID: Really, I can't imagine TJ doing something that so disappointed me. No ... I can't.

PAM: What is the scariest moment you've ever experienced onstage?

TJ: Mine was a Second City TourCo show.

DAVID: What was it?

TJ: It was a thing we did at a festival. From the tone of the show, we knew it was irrevocably screwed in the first five minutes ... and it was a fifty-minute show. It was just going to get worse as it went.

DAVID: Mine was like that too. There seems to be a key element of, "This sucks ... oh, and I've got forty more minutes ..."

TJ: ... of it getting worse. It's not even like we're going to maintain this level of suck. There is no hope of redemption. It's just going to exponentially suck more as we go.

PAM: A slow motion train wreck.

DAVID: Yeah. And it's a *fait accompli.*

PAM: There's nothing you can do to help the show.

TJ: Everything about it was nightmarish.

PAM: David, what about your scariest moment onstage?

DAVID: I learned a lot about performing from a stand-up gig I had. It was truly terrible. It was the worst possible setting, experience, my performance —everything about it was as bad as it could be. I ran out of sweat. Nothing about it was anything but horrible.

And yet … Here I am. It was helpful because when I start to get nervous, I remember, "Oh, right. I'm still going to be alive at the end of this. For better or for worse. This isn't going to kill me." I can't tell you how often I have to think of that. It's not life or death. All I can do is disappoint a few people— and really, I don't know if I can even do that by doing a terrible show. The ones looking to be disappointed will be thrilled.

PAM: … because you did disappoint them. They were right!

DAVID: And the ones who hoped I didn't eat it will, at worst, feel sorry for me. So the stakes in that regard aren't as great as possible.

Here's what really is at stake—because of my own nonsense I won't get to discover something tremendous. To paraphrase Jeffrey Sweet, I can get in the way of experiencing something wonderful right away. When I focus attention on my fear, that's the truth. This fear will prevent me from experiencing something wonderful. Why would I want that?

I think what we're getting at here is, do fail a million times. Eat it a ton. If I've never failed, that fear is huge. But if I have failed—a ton—it's just another experience I've had and survived. Why am I afraid of that?

11

DON'T STEP IN THAT: DEALING WITH TROUBLE

> The truth of the moment is another name for what is actually happening between the two people onstage. That interchange is always unplanned, is always taking place, is always fascinating ...
> — *David Mamet, True and False*

Sometimes, after a less than stellar show, an improviser steps offstage with a deep well of despair in their soul. Performing in crummy shows is part of the deal. Fortunately, it's sometimes the best way to learn some vitally important lessons. And none of that makes it feel any less like you need to scrub with a wire brush after one of those shows.

Naturally, TJ and David have performed in their share of less than stellar shows over the decades. They know what it's like to feel in trouble onstage. And they propose that perhaps the best way to deal with trouble is to redefine it.

TJ AND DAVID GET OUT OF TROUBLE

We are asked, from time to time, "How do you get yourself out of trouble?" And though we will offer a few tips for what to do and not to do when you feel like the ship is sinking, we first suggest a change of mindset about trouble in the first place.

We don't think trouble is the problem most people think it is. Yes, there are some truly shitty scenes that rear their ugly heads in improvisation now and then. Trouble does occur. We are not suggesting you pretend you're in a good scene, but it does no good to dwell on it. You fucked it up. Oops. Sit in it, commit that horrible feeling to memory and later, figure out how it happened to assure it doesn't happen again. Don't start thinking about it onstage. In a good portion of scenes where improvisers start to get that circling-the-drain feeling, they may not really be in trouble. Maybe the scene isn't going as badly as we fear. Instead of dwelling in all this self-doubt in the middle of a show, it might be helpful to shift our thinking away from the conclusion that we're in trouble in the first place.

Sometimes we sense trouble because of what we believe the audience thinks. That's crazy. First of all, it's impossible to get a read on how the audience sees the show. So don't get caught up in guessing the audience's reaction. Quite frankly, we're not very good at it. Sometimes we'll walk offstage and say, "Oooh, boy. That show was a stinker," and then someone will come up to us, effusively raving about how she has seen a ton of our shows, but that one was the best yet. Go figure. How the show is perceived is neither within our ability to understand nor is it our responsibility to do so.

Sometimes we feel in trouble because of how we believe the scene is going. The middle of a show is no place to start mucking about, making judgments about whether we're in trouble or not. To engage in that act is to fuel the problem. As Jiddu Krishnamurti said, "The ability to observe without evaluating is the highest form of intelligence." (And as TJ said of Krishnamurti, "Now that dude sounds like an improviser.") So, it seems playing to the top of our intelligence involves generous doses of non-judgment. Give up self-judgment, and you give up the ability to feel in trouble. That, in a lovely twist of fate, may get us out of the trouble we most feared.

One of the many benefits of ditching self-judgment is avoiding moves made out of fear. A common misstep that occurs when we're feeling like we just laid a rancid, slimy egg onstage is to produce a lot of exposition. We'll try to explain why what we did wasn't bad or why we were right by setting ourselves in factual ground. In the heat of the awful moment, we forget that we can rarely talk ourselves into clarity. Rather than trying to explain your way out of that hole, quiet yourselves and listen to where you currently are. (Or sidestep the whole issue by not judging the scene to be in trouble and panicking in the first place. That's an option too. Just don't fuck it up.)

Sometimes we'll see improvisers who have become uneasy with a scene resort to flailing attempts to entertain the audience by doing something silly. One time David was doing a scene with a partner who literally started dancing like a monkey, probably because he was uncomfortable. When that didn't work, he exaggerated the dancing more. Since the scene had nothing to do with dancing monkeys, no amount of monkey dancing would have helped. The only way out of Monkey Dancer's trouble would have been to do the next tiny, genuine thing—which had nothing to do with dancing like a monkey. The memory is still vivid because he's done his share of things like that. What helps is to see it from the outside and realize, 'Ohhhh ... that's what that looks like. I don't want to do that again.'"

Thinking we're in trouble, we may panic and come up with a great idea to yammer on or monkey dance our way out of the problem. Shift the main focus to avoiding self-judgment and pay attention to your onstage partner and the moment you're in, and then do the next little thing. To put it bluntly, paying attention and reacting to our stage partner with honesty is another way to keep from shitting the bed. As always, the answer to our so-called troubles is standing next to us onstage. Everything we need is in front of us. Just be truthful and respond to the little series of moments ... and lo and behold, those moments will line up into a great story. (Or not. It's fine with us either way.)

Baron's Barracudas, the 1985 ImprovOlympic Harold team, performing at CrossCurrents Cabaret. Back (l to r): Kim "Howard" Johnson, Becky Claus, John Marshall (J.J.) Jones, David Pasquesi. Front: Chris Barnes, Mark Beltzman, Honor Finnegan (not pictured, Joel Murray and Tara Gallagher). Chicago *(Courtesy of Mark Beltzman)*

David in a *God's Must Be Lazy* scene with Holly Wortell, Chris Farley and Joel Murray. The Second City, 1989. *(JenniferGirard.com)*

Young roommates, Joel Murray and David Pasquesi, met on a plane to Rome, Italy. Loyola University Rome Center, Spring, 1983.

1988 Second City Touring Company (l to r): Bill Cusack, Mark Beltzman, David Pasquesi, Brenda Varda, Joel Murray, Holly Wortell, and Tim O'Malley. *(MitchellCanoffPhotography.com)*

Flag Smoking Permitted in the Lobby Only or Censorama. The Second City, 1990.
Back row: Jill Talley, Bob Odenkirk, Chris Farley, David Pasquesi.
Front row: Tim O'Malley, Holly Wortell, Tim Meadows. *(JenniferGirard.com)*

David and Del Close in their two-man show, *Del and Dave in Rehearsal for the Apocalypse.* They also worked together in *The Chicago Conspiracy Trial.* Remains Theater, 1991. *(MitchellCanoffPhotography.com)*

David and Second City co-founder, Bernie Sahlins at the theater's 40th Anniversary, 1999. The two had a lasting friendship. *(by Michael Brosilow)*

The Gods Must be Lazy, directed by Del Close 1989. (Kumbaya scene) The Second City, 1989.
Back row: Chris Farley, Tim Meadows, David Pasquesi, Middle: Judith Scott, Joe Liss.
Front: Holly Wortell, Joel Murray. *(JenniferGirard.com)*

Set up in Charleston, S.C., with the Second City Tour Co. circa 1998. (l to r): TJ, Andy Cobb, Sue Gillan, Abby Sher, Al Samuels, and Pam Klier.

Cast of TJ's Second City Tour Co. Top: Klaus Schuller, Middle: Kristin Ford, Andy Cobb, Al Samuels, TJ Jagodowski. Front: Sue Gillan, Pam Klier.
(by Michael Brosilow)

TJ and the Second City Cast in *Psychopath Not Taken*, 1998. (l to r): TJ Jagodowski, Stephnie Weir, Rich Talarico, Susan Messing, Kevin Dorff, Tami Sagher. *(by Michael Brosilow)*

Van life with TJ and Jack McBrayer, on a Second City tour in the late '90s.

TJ with friend, Lisa (Haleski) Masseur (on right).

Carl and the Passions, TJ's long-running Harold team, circa 2000.
Top (l to r): Erin Davidson, Katie Rich, Shad Kunkle. Middle: Paul Grondy,
Jon Lutz, and TJ. Bottom: Andy St. Clair, Ellen Fox, Noah Gregoropoulos, Sue Salvi.

we aim to be in a constant state of surprise and discovery, where we don't have to make anything up; we just have to get out of the way of what is happening. We don't have to try to make it happen, we don't even have to try to *let* it happen, just step aside as it is happening. To pay attention and listen is so much easier.

Discovery is the path of least resistance, a state of not-doing and ease rather than force and effort. To us, invention (thinking up funny stuff) seems more difficult. It involves work, like an inventor toiling in a laboratory full of experiments. But discoverers? They can just stumble into the thing that's already there. We try to assume a state we call "the path of least resistance." It's a mindset to go with the simplest move. The show is a river we slip our canoe into and follow where it takes us. The path of least of resistance asks, "Why would you paddle in some other direction? Let the river take you where you need to go." We could paddle against the current (*a.k.a.* fuck up the show). Or, we can let the show take us wherever it is already going even if it leads to difficult places.

> **We have to get out of the way of what is happening.**

Energy is beautiful; effort is ugly. Energy doesn't assume resistance, but effort does. Similarly, discovery is beautiful yet invention is ugly. Also, we find it's just easier and requires less effort to join a scene, rather than invent a plot and characters in the erroneous belief that what's happening is not enough. Our job is to not introduce personal will. We simply need to allow the show to be what the show is supposed to be. And to do that, we have to pay attention to the show that is already carrying us down the river.

> **Energy is beautiful; effort is ugly.**

In one of our workshops, two students did a scene where they were waiting in line at a concert. One confessed, slightly ashamed, "I've only been to two concerts." The other one jumped on him and said, "Oh, man. That's so weird. You've only been to two concerts? That's fucked up. Two concerts?!" It was clear in how the improviser said it that he didn't believe what he was saying, but was pushing so much to make it seem odd or comedic.

We stopped the scene and suggested he not work so hard. We asked him how many concerts he had attended. "One. I saw a cover band with my parents," he replied. The example illustrates that the actual scene with the real truth would have been (and was) much more interesting than the manufactured facts. That kid worked hard to invent "funny" information rather than simply following the truth, which would have been much more entertaining and satisfying to us. And easier for him.

The idea of discovery is deceptively simple, because it seems like we're talking about doing nothing. But *not-doing* can be harder than doing. It's like falling without resisting the fall. Any attempt to make yourself safe or fight the fear destroys the possibility of improvising well, because protecting yourself requires forethought or trying to get laughs or steering the scene in the way you think it should go. Things that might lead to shelter in the real world don't lead to safety in the improvised one.

The difference between a *TJ & Dave* show and many other shows is that we believe and behave as if it's our job to discover an already-occurring scene into which we've stumbled. We noticed that the less we do, the more it seems like we are uncovering what was already happening rather than writing our own story. And those shows tend to feel pretty good. Through discovery, we stumble onto stuff that's way cooler than if we had tried to invent something new. The less pull we try to exert, story we try to tell, and scene we try to control, the more we listen to what is being said and the easier it is to follow the show. We figure that if we are following something, we must be following something pre-existing. Therefore, the scene must already exist. It isn't a magical process as much as a logical one.

Following a moment neither of us determined is one of the reasons the beginning of the show is so incredibly important for us. In *TJ & Dave*, we move from one small step to the next, the first line spoken to the next, from one moment to the next ... the whole show is just following, following, following. Miss anything at the top of the show, and we miss the opportunity to discover the scene.

Even if this pre-existing scene stuff seems like New Age nonsense, it can still work for you. When we *behave* as though the scene exists already, we find ourselves in the right frame of mind to improvise better. Stepping into a scene already "in progress" relieves the pressure to provide exposition. All we have to do is act as if we have always been these characters, as if these are the rooms we always inhabit, as if we know how we feel about each other.

Here's an example of how this process works for us from a show we will refer to as "Chill Phil:"

Lights up. Upstage right, David is seated, legs splayed out in front of him, reclined way back in a chair. TJ stands near him, looks at him and says in a tone connoting dismay and admiration, "Friggin' Chill Phil."

Phil/David replies in a chilled-out tone, "That's the way it's gotta be, man. That's the way it's gotta be." His voice pitches higher, slows, and relaxes even more. "Gots to be like that."

Laughing, TJ states, "All hell's breaking loose inside, and Chill Phil is out here just relaxing." His tone continues to be familiar and warm.

Phil/David says, "Chillaxing."

TJ asks, "You're not gonna help Ma?" Affection and knowing are clear in his voice. TJ's titling of the two characters as brothers made sense given the familial mix of affection and irritation in their relationship so far. And though he might have previously been aware of the nature of the relationship, it made sense to mention it at this point in the scene.

Phil/David says languidly and seemingly not for the first time, "If she asks."

Brother/TJ says, "Okay." He is smiling, nodding. "All right."

Phil/David continues in that very chilled-out tone, "If she asks. If she asks for my assistance, I will gladly help her."

Brother/TJ laughs. He repeats, "Okay." He seems amused and unsurprised. He knows this behavior is typical for Phil. *He acts as if he has always known this to be true.* He walks behind Phil/David and takes a seat to his right. His posture reflects Phil/David's, though a little less so. He crosses his arms. "Man!" he says shaking his head and smiling. Again, admiration, warmth, and this slight dismay fill his voice. "Man, your life. You know, she tells stories all the time," TJ takes on a woman's voice, "'Oh and then Phil— No one knew where Phil had gone ....' That's usually the second paragraph."

"Yeah, right," Phil/David slowly replies. "'And then I was worried sick' usually follows that."

Though there have not been any explicit statements beyond TJ's use of "Ma," the relationship, the dynamic, and the sense of something else happening here is clear. And is treated as it has always been clear. We act as if Phil's behavior is no surprise to either of us. It was nothing new. TJ's character approaches Phil's laziness with amusement, affection, and maybe a tiny undercurrent of irritation—an intimacy consistent with brothers. Phil's behavior is par for the course.

As improvisers in this show, we simply followed one moment to the next, making discoveries about the scene we were in. (As characters, there are no discoveries because they knew this all along.) Noticing David sitting in a relaxed way, TJ called him "Friggin' Chill Phil." David became (always was) a chillaxing guy. From TJ's fraternal reaction to Phil's chillness, it followed that Phil wasn't helping Ma in the kitchen. TJ discovered that his reaction of fondness for his brother overrode his irritation. And so on, from one discovery to the next, the scene revealed itself to us. The point is, this chillaxed guy and his brother *are enough*. It's plenty to carry us through a one-hour show.

We don't ask for suggestions at the top of *TJ & Dave*, because we don't want anything to interfere with the scene that is already happening and about to unfold. We don't feel like the audience needs that as proof of improvisation. Anyone could shoehorn a suggestion into the show they wanted to do. We just ask people to trust us: To trust that this is all made up.

> **Discovery is a quest to uncover what is already there.**

Furthermore, we mount the stage without an opening line in our heads, no emotional point of view, character ideas, or a physicality for the show. None of that comes into the scene with us. It isn't helpful. But we don't think we're starting with nothing, we believe everything we need is waiting for us on the stage. We simply need to discover what it is. As soon as the lights go up, we begin to notice, listen and observe what is already there and conveniently at hand. (The very definition of to "improvise," which is right there in David's introduction.) Discovery is a quest to uncover the pre-existing scene. At the beginning of *TJ & Dave*, two characters are finding themselves in constant reaction to a moment they've *inherited—not invented.*

Discovery in this type of improvisation involves much not-knowing and not-doing. The hard work is done. All we have to do is step onstage with the trust that we'll be fine without any of our "great" ideas. We can't force discovery because the act of trying precludes it. We only can put ourselves in a state in which we are as prepared as possible to receive it. We must let go of planning and scene steering, maintain a helpful, quiet calm, and stay in the moment with our scene partner. A sense of open receptiveness seems to help too. It's as if we're preparing for the show to be delivered to us. It is an act of faith.

That's all the mental stuff, but what are some practical things we can do to make discovery more likely? Recall that most answers lie with our stage partner. Our only help will come from the other person onstage with us and the moment between us. More specifically, our only help will come from the *relationship* we have with that other person. So keep the focus on the people in the scene. Look to your partner. Listen to your partner. Respond to your partner. Rinse. Repeat. In actionable terms, act like a human within that situation. You know, like a real person would act. Like if you were a person.

We also find it helpful to avoid getting hung up on narrative and plot. Focusing on story is the enemy of our type of improvisation. Story is a side-effect, the thing that squeezes out of the cracks if you just keep on putting people together and exploring their relationships. We find that moments end up getting strung together in sequence and create a narrative. These moments came out or were discovered because we were trying to explore what the inhabitants of the scene were going through.

We're not saying we don't include names, the environment, specifics, and details; we're just saying they're not where the crux of the scene, where the beauty of improvisation, is found. Though details may be useful, overreliance on facts, narrative, and plot obscures the most important element of the scene: the relationship between these two people here in this moment. And the nice benefit is that there is little to be remembered and much to be uncovered. By seeking the path of least resistance, we hope to make less work for ourselves, not more. In improvisation, at least as we perform it in *TJ & Dave*, there is no need to pursue the story.

In fact, we don't have to pursue anything. We continually remind ourselves that we don't have to do any of that stuff we thought we had to do. We don't have to establish the who, what, and where, create a character, or invent a plot. All will be revealed to us. We actually harm the show by inventing information and doing all that rigmarole that has nothing to do with the scene we are presently in. At first, improvisation seemed terribly confounding to us, but now we ask, "Can it be this easy?" Yes, it can—for everybody from new improvisers to the more experienced. At its best, it's easy and effortless.

Maybe you're thinking, "Screw you, TJ and Dave. I've been improvising for years, and it's not that easy. Assholes." Until we experienced it ourselves, we didn't trust that all we had to do was pay attention and do the next little thing. (Also, we are assholes.) Until you have that experience, it is unlikely you will believe it. So, give it a shot. What do you have to lose? Do a scene in which you only respond honestly and reasonably within the situation. See what happens. If it stinks to high heaven, try it again. And again. If you get to a point when you truly achieve a state of constant discovery in all your scenes, but they still stink, well, we were wrong. We will refund you the price of this book (proof required).

Want to know the real kick in the ass, the reason we safely can make that wager? Even if we can get our heads into this quiet state of not-doing, even if we focus on listening, reacting honestly, and behaving reasonably, even if we solely take the scene one step at a time, a constant state of discovery may never be achieved. It's the brass ring. The North Star. (See? We told you we were assholes.) The fact is, we have spent well over 1,000 hours onstage together merely trying to reach this state. We can only try. For we are on a quest for the impossible.

IN CONVERSATION: *DISCOVERY AND MAGIC*

Eureka!

— Archimedes

Abracadabra!

— Lots of people

In this discussion, TJ and David offer practical tips and concrete examples of how improvisers can get their heads around the concept of discovery.

PAM: During a performance, it's sometimes hard for me to tell the difference between authentically discovered moments and inventions. So how do you know when it feels right to provide new information, but not invented information born of panic or worry.

TJ: For me, the difference between the two is the feeling that it's not invented. New information feels authentic when I have reason to believe the new thing is true, based on something we already know to be true. For example, let's say it's been established that we're in a kitchen; it's not inventing to assume the next room over is a living room or a dining room. That's a logical conclusion based on facts already at hand. If someone looks kinda hungry, it's not inventing to say, "Can I make you a sandwich?" But if someone looks kinda hungry, and you say, "Oh my God, I can't believe we haven't eaten in three days. I'll make you a turkey," that feels like garbage. It's assuming or exaggerating facts that are not at hand. In both responses, you're offering someone something to eat. One feels like you're just doing the next thing, and the other feels like you're full of shit.

PAM: The second response creates a whole scenario. You're writing instead of improvising.

TJ: Inventing. Because those things weren't logically implied.

PAM: Can you expand on the idea that our only help in finding moments of discovery will come from our scene partner and the relationship between our two characters?

TJ: Your partner is pretty damn close to your only source of information as far as your relationship to them. Unless you're discovering things together, there is no real point in doing it. You rarely learn anything from crawling up inside yourself. You learn it all by paying attention to your partner, and that allows you to stay in that constant state of reaction as opposed to invention. The scene is already perfect. Our involvement raises the chance that we will fuck it up. You try to affect it as little as possible while in it.

DAVID: I was excited the first time I realized that I was being lead along, rather than driving. I'm a passenger, and I love it because all the work is done. It's thrilling to realize that I'm going to be fine, and I'm fine right now. That's the thing that I want to continue to experience. So I thought about what I had been doing when that experience happened. I realized, "Oh, I was just paying attention and doing the thing that seemed like the next thing to do." Everyone can perform as a passenger, instead of driving scenes. That's the thing that excites me.

We can get out of the way and let the show be beautiful. Or we can get in it and fuck it up. So when the show goes poorly, that's on us. And when the show goes well, we've had nothing to do with it.

> **We can get out of the way and let the show be beautiful.**
> **Or we can get in and fuck it up.**

PAM: How can I get out of the way of the show? How can I learn to follow the show? What is the actionable behavior? Do I listen and watch and so forth?

DAVID: Yeah. It's impossible to pay attention and exert my will at the same time. Try doing things we've talked about, and other things will take care of themselves. Don't actively not tell jokes. If you're paying attention, being influenced, reacting honestly, you're not going do that jokey stuff.

> **It's impossible to pay attention and exert**
> **your will at the same time.**

TJ: You can practice it if you believe it. But you have to shift your paradigm. I think most improvisers think, "We're going to do a scene now." Try shifting your thought to, "This scene is already happening," or even just, "This scene is going to happen, and now we have to go out and try not to fuck it up." The shift is from thinking you're about to go *force your will* on a scene to you're going to *stay out of the way* of the scene. You can practice it, but you have to believe that you're going about it a different way.

DAVID: I think it's the difference between "We're going to go do a scene," and "Let's go see what this is!" That's what we're asking of the audience as well. It works a lot better when everyone is uncertain but fine with it.

> It's the difference between "We're going to go do a scene,"
> and "Let's go see what this is!"

PAM: When you first get onstage, you look each other in the eye. Is that you guys tuning into the moment that's about to reveal itself?

DAVID: The "moment that's about to reveal itself" is not exactly the way we look at it. It's not *about* to do that. It's *already* doing that.

TJ: I think the eyes, if not the windows to the soul, are certainly a concentrated source of information. And they're connected to the face, which is also a good source of information ...

DAVID: ... and a communicator. Recently, we ran into a blocking problem when one person was on one side of the stage, and the other was on the opposite side. We were on the phone, and there was a little confusion because we weren't looking at one another. All the problems arise when we aren't paying attention, whether it's that we weren't paying close enough attention or things like that, just the physicality of the setting. Almost always, problems can be avoided by paying attention.

PAM: So the moment at the top of the show with the eyes is not about staring into each other's souls. It's just looking at each other.

DAVID: We're gathering as much information as we can as quickly as possible. And as TJ said, it's most focused there in the eyes. The face is the best communicator.

TJ: We're getting clues. And the best way to do that is looking at the other person. Remember, Dave, when we were doing a show way back, and we were looking out at something unseen. Was it a soccer game or something?

DAVID: Yep. We were parents watching a kids' soccer game.

TJ: We lost the top of that show to that unseen event (the soccer game). And we had nothing going on between us because we didn't look to figure that out first. We lost what we could have been to each other. I think it's human nature to think and talk about what you're looking at. And if you're looking at an invisible stove with invisible soup, you think and talk about that soup. If you look at your partner, you start thinking and talking about your partner.

DAVID: The focus of the scene is the relationship between these two people.

PAM: So that's where you look. TJ told me that you guys play around with trying to get your meaning across with as little information as possible.

DAVID: It is one of the things we do to be understood fully with almost no visible communication. Not exactly something we play around with, it's what we do all along. It's the opposite of saying, "Hello, doctor. My spleen is still bothering me, even though I was here last week."

PAM: Instead of all that premise-based narrative at the top.

DAVID: The exact opposite of that. In a show, it can be all understood. It happens really fast, without even a word. Nobody else would see it. Sometimes even people onstage with us don't see it because they're not looking for it. But we are.

TJ: If you're looking for gold, you're more likely to find it than if you're not looking for it.

DAVID: Sometimes we see if we can do even less. Sometimes we miss. Sometimes it wasn't enough. In rock climbing, when wondering how tight to hold onto the rock, they advise to grip the rock one more than falling off. That's kind of what we're trying to do. We want to be understood but without any excess.

TJ: It's a little added challenge element. Sometimes it comes up. Sometimes it doesn't. I think, "What's the tiniest part of this that I can do or say that still is crystal clear to Dave but is closer to atomic in size than atomic bomb?"

DAVID: It would be crystal clear to me but kind of looks like magic to anyone else.

TJ: We *will* get the message across. It's a bonus if nobody sees you do it. Instead of saying, "Hello, doctor. I'm still having problems with my spleen," you can say, "Same old *bullshit*." And still get all that across. If I said that, David still would know that I'm a patient, and he's a doctor. If it's not the spleen, then it's right in this section of his body, so it's more likely to be a spleen. With "Same old bullshit," all that information is conveyed.

DAVID: Even the doctor's response—"How's your golf game?"—has a whole bunch of other stuff in there.

PAM: That scene looks like:

> TJ/PATIENT *[indicating to his abdomen]*: Same old *bullshit*.
>
> DAVID/DOCTOR: How's your golf game?

Does the other guy always get it? Would you know that you're in a doctor's office, David?

DAVID: If he's sure of it, I'll probably get it. That's a big part, to be sure of it.

TJ: And if by chance, we're not on exactly on the same page, then we'll leak out a little more info. But at first, we see if we can get away with as little as possible. Would you say that's right, David?

DAVID: Absolutely.

TJ: Since we're looking at each other, we'll see in each other's eyes if that bit of information just leaked out, and if it registered or not.

DAVID: And the truth is, we're probably both learning this at the same time during the scene. If I had been the patient, I wouldn't be walking onstage with a spleen problem in my doctor's office. I just wouldn't. It's more that I am here with this guy, so I try to figure out, "What does this seem like? Who do we seem to be? Where are we?"

That little bit at a time being leaked out is probably 100% of what I know.

TJ *[laughing]*: It's a drop, but it's my entire scope of knowledge.

DAVID: Right. It's minute. But it's plenty!

PAM: That way, you don't have to change anything or concede anything because you didn't have the whole doctor's office scenario in mind when you walked onstage. You just had this complaint.

TJ: And that follow-up comment to the patient, "How's your golf game?" There is a *ton* of information in that. If Dave's trying to convey "doctor" with that, that's exactly what I'll get. And I'll get his disdain. I'll get the fact that he thinks I'm a man of leisure and that I haven't been following his doctor's orders because I'm too busy worrying about my backswing. All that information can be in that one line—a who, a where, and really important information that applies to our relationship. That this patient hates that he has to come to this doctor. He needs the doctor and has absolute contempt for him all at the same time.

PAM: Setting up the who, the what, the where at the top doesn't help you to create an interesting, sustainable scene as much as those few comments, like "Same old *bullshit.*"

DAVID: Our task is to try to figure out what scene is here already, not what scene we brought in.

PAM: During our *Geeking Out with* ... interview, TJ said: "What Dave and I consider to be a really good show is when this element of magic happens that feels like neither of us determined, that neither of us made happen. We just happened to be visited by this extra thing that was going on that night. In our jargon, there is no better term for it than 'magic' happening." Is the state of discovery another key to the "magic" of *TJ & Dave*?

DAVID: Only in that when we are in the mindset of discovery rather than invention, this other thing occurs.

TJ: *May* occur. We're giving ourselves, hopefully, a higher possibility of being visited by this other thing.

DAVID: We're setting the table. We're trying to create the conditions to allow that to happen again.

PAM: Do you perceive it as magic?

DAVID: Not anymore. Magic is something that confounds me. But with our show, I have actually come to expect it. There is me. And there is TJ. And there is something between us, which is also a real thing. Magic? Sure.

TJ: We as humans are pretty great lie detectors. When we get a bad read, we're around one hell of a liar or more likely deluding ourselves. If Dave and I are paying very close attention, we can create certain illusions; magic is the thing we can't account for.

PAM: You're saying there is a difference between an illusion, which can be created by crazy amazing listening, and then there is something else altogether that seems like magic?

TJ: I'm saying Dave and I try to do everything we possibly can to welcome it, to prepare for a visit. Sometimes it arrives. Sometimes it doesn't.

PAM: Like magic.

13

HEAT AND WEIGHT

The aim of life is to live, and to live means to be aware,
joyously, drunkenly, serenely, divinely aware.
— *Henry Miller*

Pay attention to the frog. Pay attention to the west wind.
Pay attention to the boy on the raft, the lady in the tower, the old
man on the train. In sum, pay attention to the world and all that
dwells therein and thereby learn at last to pay attention to yourself
and all that dwells therein.
— *Frederick Buechner*

Often, improvisers are told to start their scene in the middle with characters who already know each other, in order to avoid "Hi, my name is ..." introductions or starting in a once-upon-a-time fashion. How do you do that without sounding artificial and contrived? Who wants a scene that begins overly explicitly, such as "As my sister, you should know that ever since Dad moved out, we're barely scraping by"? Such an opening line seems like a gift in order to make the rest of the scene easy to play. But what if you're not the sister?

In real life, we behave as though the nature of the relationship is self-evident. So why wouldn't we do that onstage? TJ and David perform as if the scene existed before they took the stage and will continue well after they leave it. They are stepping into their characters' real lives for fifty or so minutes, and the challenge is to assess whose lives they're living while maintaining the existing reality of those lives. To that end, they've developed their own vocabulary and approach to assessing the moment they're in, which they refer to as the "Heat" and the "Weight."

TJ AND DAVID DEFINE THE CONCEPTS

The sisterly example up there may sound like a very generous and thoughtful beginning to a scene. It certainly is a beginning where you need not find out any of those onerous details because they are presented to you right up front. Now you know all those things and all you have to do is play them. Easy, huh? Well, the way we see it, "As my sister, you should know that since Dad moved out, we're barely scraping by ..." is neither easy nor considerate. Because now we're being told that we are that person's sister even though our behavior up to that point may have been inconsistent with being a sister. Now we have to rationalize why we were behaving like a 40-year-old male drill sergeant for that little bit at the top because that's no longer true. Sure, we could do that justification, but why should we have to? Why not just play the truth of the scene that actually is going on?

These instances are where the concepts we call Heat and Weight can be of use. They are our shorthand for quickly getting a read on what's going on at the top of a scene. Heat is the intimacy and intensity of the relationship—anything from complete strangers standing next to each other on a train to soul mates who have been married for fifty years. Weight refers to what is already in the room; what it feels like is going on. Beginning a *TJ & Dave* show, we try to open ourselves up to the Heat and the Weight. How? We listen with our whole selves.

You could think of Heat in reference to the "temperature" of the relationship. Envision looking through heat-sensing glasses at an animal slowly approaching you on an African savannah. You might not be able to tell the difference between a hyena and a goat, but you will know that it's so big and so tall. You may not know the exact animal, but you'll definitely know it's not a lion stalking prey or an elephant on a rampage. A look at your scene partner will do the same thing. We may not know if our scene partner is our sister, husband, or long time mentor, but with one mindful look, we can tell if the person has a deep and genuine concern for us. We can see it in expression, posture, and proximity. He is looking into our eyes with warm caring. There is an upward tilt to his mouth. His arms relax at his sides, palms facing out as if ready to catch us if we fall. Just by reading the Heat of the relationship in that first second, we know this person wants to help, not eviscerate us. And now our education has begun. Now we know there is an intimate Heat to our relationship.

Heat is the intimacy and intensity of the relationship.

Conversely, that same first glance at our scene partner might quickly tell us that it's a total stranger staring back at us. Her eyes don't register our presence. After a quick glance in our direction, she goes back to looking at her phone. Her expression doesn't suggest any particular emotion. Her body is facing away from us. The Heat of that relationship is tepid. In either of these scenarios, we have learned a lot already about our relationship from that one moment of paying attention.

Determining the Heat of the scene calls upon common instincts. Most of us are hardwired to use non-verbal cues to quickly assess the intimacy of relationships. Since we're trying to capture the truth of real life onstage, why wouldn't we use the same real life skills? At a café, you may see two people across the room having what appears to be a polite, somewhat formal conversation. You may guess that they're two people who used to be friends, but now have nothing in common, or perhaps they're mildly acquainted business associates. What's clear is they have no strong bonds or feelings between them. We'd say both those relationships have a similar Heat. On the other hand, you've probably noticed that hot and heavy couple at the corner table in the back, both flushed, laughing, locked on, as though no one else exists. By the way they're looking at each other, you can feel an entirely different Heat.

Beware the danger of confusing the *title* of a relationship—parent/child, boss/worker, husband/wife—with the specific Heat of a relationship. There are father/son relationships that have the Heat of casual drinking buddies. And there are father/son relationships that have the Heat of sworn enemies. Some student/teacher relationships have the Heat of chess partners, while others have the Heat of jilted lovers. As we see it, the relationship is not the title, but rather the strength of the emotional connection between people. At the top of the show, we try to determine the intensity of the relationship between us, and play that Heat rather than worrying about whatever exact title our relationship may be. Although it's virtually impossible to discern the title of a relationship from a brief glance at the beginning of a scene, it is quite possible to get pretty good at determining the Heat. By paying close attention to the Heat at the top of a show, we avoid situations such as one of us thinks we're a devoted husband and wife while the other thinks we're complete strangers at a bus stop. Those totally different Heats cannot possibly both be true given how we'd already been behaving. We trust that our reads will be similar enough that the details won't matter. The level of our intimacy is what's important, not the name we put on it. And all of this information starts to be conveyed in our first look at each other when the lights go up.

> **The relationship is not the title, but the strength of the emotional connection between people.**

The other unspoken thing going on in our quick assessment at the top of the scene we've popped into is the Weight, which is the other unspoken thing going on. Whereas Heat applies to the intensity and intimacy of the *relationship*, Weight applies to the import and tone of the *situation* in which we find ourselves. You know when you walk into a place and you instantly get the sense of, "Uh oh. Some serious stuff just went down in here," and your instinct is to back slowly out of the room before they see you? That's what we call the Weight. It's the thing already in the room with us. What is the energy in the scene? *How* is the first line being delivered? What is the feeling being transmitted? What is our emotional reaction to that feeling? The way a person is looking at our character and the feeling it evokes in us gives clues to the Weight of the situation.

> **Weight refers to what is already in the room with you.**

Imagine the look of your closest loved one who is concerned that you have become hooked on pills. Even before they say anything, you can tell there's a pretty fair amount of Weight in the room. Now imagine the look of that same loved one's mild concern about you, as if you're overdue for a shower and haircut. That one is less Weighty. That initial read places a different Weight, an unspoken feeling, in the room with us.

A look of concern about a pill addiction places a similar Weight in a scene as someone who is concerned their spouse is about to ask for a separation. Both of those looks convey a worry that their loved one will be removed from them. They're both pretty heavy. Initially, we're okay with this type of ambiguity. At the top of the scene, we are not primarily concerned about naming the relationship, giving the situation a title, or labeling the situation that exists between these two people. We do not feel the need to define our Heat and Weight immediately by saying something like "Hey, Sis, it's time to go to rehab." Or, "Please don't throw away our twenty-five years of marriage, babe." That feels too clumsy and unrealistic. Instead, we notice the Heat and Weight, assume we have assessed it correctly (until proven otherwise), and behave as if our assessment is given fact. Paying attention to that first look is essential. It may silently convey that five seconds before the lights came up, one person said the foulest thing the other person has ever heard, and we better hide the sharp objects. Or, maybe, one person said the foulest thing the other person has ever heard but they loved it, sexy-style. Either of the two vastly different Weights may be true, but only one is. The only way to find out is by paying close attention.

> **We notice the Heat and the Weight, assume we have assessed them correctly and behave as if our assessment is given fact.**

Remember, the scene begins with what we have onstage—each other and what is happening between us. We must immediately begin our process of looking and listening. Looking. Listening. Then after we've gotten a first read on the Heat and Weight, our education continues. A line may be spoken with affection and gentle chiding, such as "Friggin' Chill Phil." A little later, a name may be given to the relationship or to the thing in the room, which is great as long as it fits with the Heat and Weight already established. Or maybe the relationship won't be labeled directly. Even if we've never said we're brothers, hopefully, from the way we're behaving, it becomes pretty clear. In that "Chill Phil" scene we described a while back, you may recall that eventually TJ said, "You gonna help Ma?" putting a title on the relationship, not solely to label it but also because it fits with the nature of the relationship.

> **The secret is not to respond to the words being spoken, but to the emotion being evoked beneath those words.**

The secret is not to respond to the words being spoken, but to the emotion being evoked beneath those words. In the example above, we don't need to question why one of us is so chill or if we're brothers. Once felt, noticed, then declared, it becomes fact. Right away, we know these are guys are on the same side of whatever is going on—even though Phil is not helping their mom, it's not a surprise or even a big deal. (That's a nice chunk of information about the Heat right there.) That reality now exists and need not be discussed or disputed or justified.

We don't find it helpful to get caught up in words, providing a lengthy exposition at the top of a scene. When improvisers produce a lot of narrative at the start, they're trying to make sure the audience is on the same page. But we believe the audience is already there; and even if they aren't, they couldn't care less about narrative. The audience finds emotional relationships more compelling than a plot outline. They don't care that we're brothers who haven't seen each other in a while, and we're getting ready for dinner at our parents' home. They are more drawn into a scene about the discovered relationship between a shiftless slacker/prodigal son and his home-/duty-bound brother. Or if the audience isn't, at least we are.

To us, the show is about the exchange of emotions. So we listen to the message being conveyed by our scene partner's tone of voice, expression, body language, proximity, etc. as well as the emotional message we are transmitting to our scene partner in the same ways. Everything right there in front of us is material to examine and react to as we take the next little step in the scene. And those reactions provide new material to which we listen intently and react reasonably. We assess the Heat and the Weight as we attempt to solve the mystery of who we are to each other and what is going on between us. We try to respond to each other in a way that is natural and logical. If all goes well, by the end of the show, it seems like we simply slipped into the reality that was there when the lights came up.

It's at this point in the show that we apply the principles of Ockham's razor, which has two elements: 1.) Plurality should not be posited without necessity, and 2.) It is pointless to do with more what is done with less. Medieval philosopher William of Ockham apparently employed the theory that the most likely explanation is probably the simplest one, unless there is proof of something more elaborate. In other words, if it looks like a duck, swims like a duck, and quacks like a duck, then it's probably a duck. Or, if you see hoof prints in your front yard, you should first assume horse rather than zebra (to be treated conversely if you live in the savannahs of Africa). Or, if your scene partner approaches with a pleasant expression, assume she is friendly and not a serial killer who wants to sleep in your skin (until proven otherwise). As a scene is developing, we try to assume the most obvious explanation consistent with what's already occurred. We are both knowingly applying Ockham's razor to the scene by assuming the obvious explanation, which gives us another possibility to wordlessly, and sometimes seamlessly, figure out together what scene is being revealed to us.

> **As a scene is developing, we try to assume the most obvious explanation consistent with what's already occurred in the scene.**

The lights go up. We look at our scene partner. Then we use our natural instincts and observational powers to determine the Heat and Weight of the scene. We must trust that our assessments are correct, that our assumptions about the Heat of the relationship and the Weight of the situation in which we find ourselves are utterly on target. *This is an act of faith.* We trust that even though we might not have exactly the same details or title of who we are to each other or what's already in the room, our reads of the Heat and Weight are congruent. We trust that our shared Heat formula of "loyal frat brothers" equals "devoted secretary and boss" is correct. And the Weight of "We just escaped from white-collar prison" or "We just flew through a dangerous thunderstorm" is also equivalent. It works because we trust our scene partner implicitly ... and we've practiced it a lot. When rehearsing *TJ & Dave,* we mainly run the tops of scenes then discuss them in order to get as adept as possible at synchronizing our Heat and Weight assessments. This way, once we get onstage, there doesn't need to be a huge leap of faith, but rather a steady confidence that our reads are consistent with each other.

Performers often think, "There's no way I can know this whole Heat and Weight thing at a glance. My assessment sucks, and my partner probably knows it." We all have doubts, but guess what? You *can* know it. You *do* know it. Have faith. We practice assessing Heat and Weight, but we also practice trusting we are correct in our assessments. Why wouldn't we? To do anything else is to trust we're wrong. And that's not helpful to anyone.

Rest easy; none of us do this instant assessment perfectly or even very well every time. That's okay. The point is that we can get better. We need to embrace this whole endeavor as a process of improving, learning, and not knowing it all. Improvisation is something you can enjoy wildly while you're doing it and, at the same time, know "Hey, I'm not very good at this yet." (It's like sex in this way.) The goal is to commit fully and trust in our partners. A good idea before taking the stage is to remind oneself and all involved that the goal is not to be funny or to be clever. The goal is to be present.

IN CONVERSATION: *FIRST MOMENTS OF A SHOW*

TJ & Dave shows always begin with "Trust us, this is all made up." Black out. When the lights rise, TJ and David are looking at each other. Remarkably, over one thousand of these identical beginnings have resulted in over one thousand radically different stories.

In a performance captured in their documentary, *Trust Us, This is All Made Up*, TJ and David are center stage, near one other when the lights come up. TJ starts nodding, and he seems to have an expression of friendly reassurance.

The nodding continues until TJ says, "You'll bounce back, man. You'll bounce back."

With a neutral expression, David raises his hand in a "stop" signal. He shakes his head a little and replies in a deep voice, "I don't want to get into it."

TJ continues kind encouragement, "Yeah, you'll bounce back though." He puts a hand on his hip, the other on the chair. "Tough day," he says. Their opening dialogue is unhurried and patient. TJ continues, "Breathe through it. Isn't that what they say? Breathe through it. Breathe into it. You know when you're getting a rubdown and it hurts? Breathe into it—"

"Breathe into the area that is bringing you pain? Yeah." David's voice is quick and clipped with an edge to it.

"Breathe into it. Yeah, breathe into it, man." TJ's consistent expression has a small smile of support and encouragement. He gestures with his head towards an area behind David. "You could hear some of the screaming from out here."

David interrupts with the same emotional voice, "Hey, look. I say what I need to say. That's what I do."

Underneath comes TJ's continued reassurance, "Yeah, absolutely."

David plows on passionately, "You know what happens when you keep it in? When you keep it in ... cancer."

"Right, yeah," says TJ, "like Jackie Robinson."

"Yeah, right!" exclaims David. "Right! Right!"

The Heat and Weight of the situation they stepped into become increasingly clear. Over the next fifty minutes, step by step, they reveal a show whose foundation was discovered and established in those first few moments.

PAM: Can you walk us through the key moments of that beginning?

TJ: Like always, we get a read on the scene. In *Trust Us,* by his posture, it looked like Dave was down or coming off something not great. That was all I knew of him, and I felt like I was in a sympathetic posture.

The first look felt like we were friends. He didn't look at me like we were strangers, so to the best of my knowledge we were friends or at least friendly. Dave, though maybe slightly upset, was not upset at me. And if we were friends, I would be rooting for him, and so I said, "You'll bounce back."

PAM: So how did you see the Heat?

TJ: The Heat would be pretty medium in *Trust Us.* There was an affinity but not much intensity.

PAM: And how did you determine that? Body language? Eyes? A feeling?

DAVID: It's all of that. It's all determined through paying attention. TJ was looking at me, looking supportive, nodding, encouraging. His posture was not at all dominant. He looked like he felt maybe a little sorry for me. Or maybe a little bit guilty. From that, I got that I am more dominant, and either something just happened to me, or I did something. The Heat is "friends." (So far.) It may change somewhat, but I am pretty sure we are not lovers passionately involved in a tryst.

The first words, "You'll bounce back, man. You'll bounce back," further establish what was already pretty clear: he was offering encouragement. From the way he said it, it seemed he might not fully believe it. But what was clear is that he was trying to help me, whoever I am. Therefore, I knew I must be his friend because that is how friends behave toward one another.

TJ: And that's why I would say that Heat is medium.

PAM: Is that how you saw the Heat, David?

DAVID: I think the gradation of Heat is not as useful as recognizing that we should be looking for Heat and Weight—but not trying to give them a score of, say, an eight or a four. It's more important to recognize the existence of the Heat and Weight rather than the relationship's title and other factual matters.

The magic of this approach is that we can actually know this stuff. People don't believe that these things can be communicated, but they can. People think the only things that we can be certain of are the little facts we declare, but those things simply are not interesting or helpful.

TJ: That sounds good, David.

PAM: You two have a special non-verbal connection, which makes this type of assessment easier. I'm not saying other improvisers are not capable of doing it, but it would be nice to have some breadcrumbs laid out here to guide the way.

DAVID: Practice. Try it. See what happens.

Just look at one another in the comfort of a rehearsal. One person should have something in mind, very specific. For example, I am a third grader being reprimanded for showing up late for class, but the teacher doesn't know I was helping a lady change a tire. See how much gets communicated by only looking at one another, using no words—though it's not a dumb show (not mime nor charades). Just silently look at one another with a clear understanding of a very particular situation.

PAM: That is a fascinating rehearsal exercise. Since you told me about it, I've tried it a bunch of times. It's pretty amazing how much can be communicated by just paying attention and reading body language.

It's truly remarkable that all the Heat and Weight information you assessed at the top of *Trust Us* carried you through the entire fifty minutes. You invented very little additional information, which continually astounds me.

TJ: More information comes with each proceeding moment.

DAVID: And it doesn't carry us through fifty minutes. It carries us to the next moment.

PAM: Points taken. Though, over the duration of the show, you stuck with the information initially revealed.

DAVID: Yes, because it isn't fiction. It is the truth. We can figure out what is happening and then behave accordingly. It isn't a bunch of lies. Lies are impossible to keep straight. The truth is; we don't even have to keep it straight.

PAM: Eventually, you start to discuss the other thing in the room, the Weight. In *Trust Us*, you begin to suspect that something bad just went down in the other room. How do you sense that?

TJ: It was already there. It's what made Dave look the way he did at the top, and me too. We just don't know the name of it yet. We know it's lighter than Dave losing a child and heavier than there being too few peanuts in his snack bag. Environment plays in, with it being a corporate setting. Clues are coming in a lot of different ways. We keep playing the level of Weight until a name is put to it. In *Trust Us*, the name was "an argument over a softball team."

DAVID: When TJ said, "You'll bounce back," it seemed to me that this was the first time we had seen one another since some unnamed incident. These were TJ's first words to me since then. We are friends and, seemingly, we see a lot of one another. It felt kinda workplace-y, so it follows that this just occurred at work. Also, if this thing did just occur at work, it does not make anything we've already established wrong.

"You'll bounce back." Hearing this, I know something happened that I might need to bounce back from. We believe the information is all true. We are not going along wondering if it's true. We go through the scene, "This is true ... This is true ... This is true ... This is also true ... Now this is true ...."

PAM: You're gathering clues and accepting them as fact. The idea that you keep playing the level of Weight until a name is put to it is fascinating. While you have said that Heat can be based primarily on observable facts and clues, Weight seems less concrete and more ... *feeling* ...

DAVID: Yes.

PAM: Can an improviser utilize the practice of assessing Heat and Weight in a scene with other improvisers who are not familiar with the concept? Is the idea that this practice is easier with two people who understand it, agree, and trust?

DAVID: It's not just easier, it's essential. It is impossible without those criteria met.

TJ: I would say I use it in some form in just about every scene I do. But often in shows outside *TJ & Dave*, a Heat or Weight is already established by form or established less organically.

DAVID: You can use this technique but not to great effect, unless all participants do it. Of course, I evaluate, read, and understand scenes and relationships this way all the time. Some folks don't trust this, and they change the truth as the scene continues. That's tough. It's hard to deal with that, with the truth changing.

TJ and I do not change the truth. The other day in a show, I sat in an imaginary car. The steering wheel was very far from me, my arms extended.

So instead of pretending that I hadn't established or noticed that and simply made the steering wheel closer, I adjusted my seat, sliding it closer to the steering wheel. That gave us more information about why the seat was back. A delightful accident and a mistake.

PAM: I saw that show! You were playing cops getting into your squad car. TJ's character was holding an overly full coffee cup, trying not to spill. When David got into the car, he noticed his arms extended way out to hold the steering wheel. And that lead him to comment on why TJ kept the seats so far back in the car. TJ's character revealed he sometimes slept in the backseat of the car, and that he liked the seats pulled back so it "felt like a womb." That moment was informative, and it led to the establishment of another dimension in your characters and relationship.

Even more remarkable, the next day, out of nowhere, David laughed recalling that moment because he was surprised to have found the steering wheel so far away. Surprising yourself is a goal in improvisation, it seems to me.

DAVID: Absolutely. And you cannot be surprised if you already know.

TJ: And if David "already knew" the steering wheel to be too far away, it would have read as a planned bit. If we think we already know who we are or what is going on, it will read that way, or one could be tempted to shove that idea forward at the expense of what is actually happening.

DAVID: We are just talking about a tiny thing like bad object work here. Imagine if we were to treat Heat and Weight the same way, as being true to what is established. In *Trust Us*, it was established that TJ felt sorry for me and wanted to help out. Maybe he is not sure how or if he can do anything for me. Nevertheless, I am affected by his efforts.

PAM: So in relation to the *Trust Us* scene, you used this process to assess everything—the Heat, the Weight, the environment ...

TJ: It felt like an office based on the clues. It would only screw us or look cute or clever if we try to make it a Russian sub.

DAVID: Damn. That would have been funny, a Russian sub.

TJ: Right after I said it, I wished it were a Russian sub.

DAVID: TJ does a great Russian sub commander character who only says, "Da!" real loudly. It's *hilarious*. He drinks vodka but doesn't like the taste. His daughter is a real disappointment. She banged an American on holiday and had a bastard child.

TJ: I also do another Russian commander, but he drinks tequila.

PAM: So, "keep it simple, stupid" when it comes to assessing Heat and Weight?

TJ: Only because it's easier.

DAVID: The goal is not to be clever. The goal is to be honest, and not because it is better (though it is). The goal is to be honest just because, as TJ says, it is easier.

TJ: I would say it's even more important near the top. Things are likely going to get a little odder or more show-specific as the time goes. There is no need to force all that in the beginning. Without a strong foundation and a believable start, you can't build to a more idiosyncratic world because idiosyncratic is all it's ever been.

PAM: Would you say that you do look toward the established reality when moving forward?

DAVID: I do not look back. I try to react honestly in each moment in accordance with the established truth. That is different than looking back.

PAM: While the Heat and Weight of the scene are revealing themselves, you don't recommend using the first lines of the scene to ask why the other person is feeling the way he is. For instance, you said, "You'll bounce back" rather than, "Why are you so upset?"

TJ: The "why" will take you on a fact-finding mission, which may answer a question but provides zero information on the relationship. I would say it's more useful to see how you are together when someone feels the way they do. Dig into relationship. The fact that when one is sad, both of you cry is more useful than knowing why someone is sad.

PAM: So, "why" threatens to lead to the creation of narrative at the top of the scene, which isn't useful in discovering the emotional relationship. How can improvisers best learn to stick to the information discovered at the top of a scene?

TJ: I guess you just have to not freak out. A lot of extra material gets added or laid on because you're afraid what's already there isn't enough. It's just a matter of believing that you have done enough. You are doing enough. You don't have to invent stuff that isn't already there, or we don't have a reason to believe is already there.

PAM: I like the idea that the scene already exists, that even the end of the scene is already onstage with you. You're merely stepping into it.

TJ: It's the idea of letting the beginning take you to the next moment to the next to the next, which will bring you to what appears like the ending that already was. But you need to follow the thread step by step as opposed to knowing that the "John, can you come into my office?" scene ends in a firing.

DAVID: The end is not a concern. Following the thread is the job.

TJ: As a show progresses, the Heat and Weight become more defined. They may intensify or wane. Other characters enter, introducing new Heats and Weights and affecting the existing Heats and Weights. All this sounds complicated, but is much easier when you just go moment to moment, paying attention.

DAVID: Right. The end of the scene is not my responsibility or concern. Just this moment. And that person right there. I don't have to pay attention to the facts, I should be paying attention to things like Heat and Weight.

PAM: So you are talking about an acutely moment-by-moment assessment and listening/reaction process. Performed honestly.

TJ: Welcome to the party, dummy!

PAM: Ha! Nice joke, TJ.

TJ: What joke?

14

TAKING THE NEXT LITTLE STEP

*Faith is taking the first step even when you don't see
the whole staircase.*
— Reverend Doctor Martin Luther King, Junior
*(not to be confused with the leader of the Protestant Reformation,
Martin Luther) (also not to be confused with the religiously
unaffiliated Doctor Martin Luther Kung, who is a back specialist)*

The ideas of "taking the next little step" and "approaching the scene moment by moment" are the very heart of their guiding principle "Always behave and respond honestly in the moment." TJ and David perform with the understanding that they are discovering the scene into which they have stepped, and their only job is to respond honestly. They don't think three steps out, or aim towards an assumed conclusion, and they especially do not set up a funny joke. They simply take the next little step. The next logical step. Not until all the steps have been walked do they look at how those moments pieced together as a show.

Their approach is simple in theory, but there is a great deal of letting go that some performers might need to do when improvising one little step at a time. Practicing this type of improvisation may feel like going against some of your training. But if you're so inclined, read on, then round up some like-minded folks and try it out.

TJ AND DAVID ELABORATE ON FAITH

Here's a little quote, supposedly said by a wise woman: "Faith is not jumping from point A to point B. Faith is jumping from point A." In improvisation, we constantly are taking this leap of faith, jumping from point A into thin air.

On the bright side, we are not supposed to know what or where point B is, nor are we expected to know. We are just supposed to jump. As Ray Bradbury famously advised writers, "Jump off cliffs as I do and build your wings on the way down. No blueprints, no plans. Just jump."[1]

Sometimes improvisers try to speed their education of the moment and the specifics of the scene they're playing. Early in a scene, they might assume they know more than they do in an attempt to provide a safe place for themselves. But we have a different relationship with not knowing. We see it as part of a package deal with improvisation, so we might as well embrace it. We don't have to know anything until we do know—until brows furrow, a smile cracks, eyes twinkle, and a piece of information reveals itself. And even then we don't know everything, just one little piece of the path. We only need to watch closely for what is revealed, and then take the next little step.

> **The plain truth is that everything we need is in front of us.**
> **All we have to do is find out what it already is.**

Though improvisation can seem complicated, this is a confoundingly simple approach. The plain truth is that everything we need is in front of us. We have to find out what it already is. Let some unknown thing unfold one tiny moment at a time. No plans. No great scene ideas or stories. Just the next little tiny thing.

"What?!" you may be yelling at the book. "How do I even *know* what step to take out of the multitudes of possible steps?"

First of all, "Stop yelling at the book. Come on, man. It's a book. Its biggest crime is a paper cut. (Or if you're on your tablet, a virtual paper cut.)"

The lights go up. We Listen. We Pay Attention. We assess and explore the Heat and Weight. We don't know how or when it's all going to end, so we don't pretend we do. Improvisation is itself an exercise in faith ... in faith of Improvisation. That if we do the next tiny thing, all will be fine.

Let's evaluate the beginning of a show we call *You've Gotten So Asian*. At lights up, David was stretching, perhaps bowing, as he bent over touching his toes. TJ was sitting in a chair stage right. From somewhere offstage, probably the bar, we could hear a clear-toned ding of a glass being hit. Maybe it sounded a little like one of those singing bowls.

---

(1) Bradbury, Ray. *Bradbury Speaks: Too Soon from the Cave, Too Far from the Stars*. New York: William Morrow, 2005.

Improvisation is itself an exercise in faith, in the faith of Improvisation. That if we do the next tiny thing, all will be fine.

David remembers, "I was bending over. I noticed I was bending over. I saw TJ watching me bend. I bent more. I was bending at the waist, and TJ was watching me. He was sitting. I bent more … that's what seemed to be going on, which is *plenty*. (In fact, I was truly stretching my back. Boy, that feels good …)

Then TJ said, 'You've gotten so Asian.' I noticed the way he said it, not only the words. In fact, the words were not nearly as important as what else was communicated by those four words. Maybe he was looking up to me. Maybe he was a lady. Maybe he was impressed with me. It seems like he was saying that from a seat of not being Asian. Now that's a lot of maybes, so why not make them certainties? That's more helpful. Has anything happened that denies these things? No. Then they are true. (Until they're not.)"

Once our somewhat objective assessment of the Heat and Weight has taken place, we're full participants. We become active players in the scene as we react to and are affected emotionally by our stage partner. Taking things step by step, we don't need to spend time talking about (and reassuring ourselves) who these characters are and what they are doing. We can merely notice who they are and what they are doing, treat it as fact, and move on. When we assume it's true, we don't have to explain why or how David has gotten so Asian. He has gotten so Asian—that's now fact—so what's the next step? We'll best find it by noticing and exploring how these characters feel about each other.

We are not there to serve the plot. We are there to serve the relationship.

When taking the next little step, we always look to the relationship. We find the dynamic between people to be endlessly fascinating. Everything else—the plots, the facts, the characters, are all there to support the relationship. We are not there to serve the plot. We are there to serve the relationship.

David picks up his deconstruction of *You've Gotten So Asian*: "It seemed that TJ was familiar to me. The way he said 'You've gotten so Asian' suggested he was not Asian, and that there had been a change and distance between us.

Now that I know some things, what do I do? I could wait until I get further proof that my assumptions are corroborated, but that is boring and wasteful and disrespectful to TJ. So I merely behave honestly within the established reality. In fact, he is certain I *have* become quite Asian. I didn't feel ashamed of it. It is a change from a previous me, or he wouldn't have said it. These are now facts."

Just to be clear, we're not saying that there is one universal truth that applies to all the characters in the scene. Each of us maintains our point of view. It is a fact that TJ felt David was becoming more Asian, and David had the freedom to decide how he felt about it. Turns out, he was not ashamed. That became a fact too.

Not only do we allow our stage partner this freedom of choice, but we also show respect by assuming they are well-informed. In moving from one moment to another, we always accept that our stage partner is correct and that his behavior is consistent with who he is. When taking the next little step, it's simply easier to accept they're right rather than to wonder if they're lying or to fight with them about the reality of the scene. We treat everything as real and nothing as manufactured or invented since we arrived at these conclusions through actual data. We're not spinning fantasies or wishes. We're making logical conclusions based on the reality of the scene that exists already.

In the show that we just described, the first moments were completed in silence, aside from TJ's one remark. Remember, we are aiming to speak as poets onstage ... we surely won't get there, but at the very least, we can try to be judicious in our approach to words. Maybe the next little step is a gesture, a moment of reaction, or a movement. TJ recalls one next little thing David did in a recent show, "He moved just the tiniest bit closer to me and leaned in as if possibly expecting a kiss. It was a silent three inch move that spoke volumes." We keep in mind that the next little thing might be not saying anything at all.

Notice we haven't said the next little step has anything to do with heightening anything in the scene. (If you're unfamiliar with the term, "heightening" refers to the act of escalating the intensity of an element in a scene. For example, we learn that a man is nervous about the upcoming birth of his child and someone tags in as an Ob/Gyn and says it's quadruplets. Or in a scene between two women, one says she is just out of a rough relationship with a guy and, after a few minutes, the other woman reveals she just started seeing that same guy.) For our show, we find the usual use of heightening typically too artificial and contrived. Rather than play only one intensified element of the scene, we choose to play the actual scene, the relationship.

Perhaps when we look back after the show, we may realize there might have been some emotional heightening that occurred naturally over the course of the show. Or maybe not. But that's not where we put our energy.

We don't even use the term or concept of "heightening," which usually looks like artificially turning up the dial on an energy level. Instead, we find the idea of *developing* more useful. As in a darkroom, a photograph develops; it becomes clear and specific. That doesn't happen from heightening. Rather than thinking of it as increasing any single element, we consider this process as revealing the characters and their relationships.

TJ takes an example from the aforementioned show and explains, "At the top of the show, I am someone who says, 'You've gotten so Asian.' I would stay open to developing that character, remaining true to how the audience first met him but becoming *more* of that as the show goes. And that's going to happen if I just allow that character to develop through the information I receive from David and the show. It's not getting bigger or doubling the energy. It's just maintaining the commitment to who that character is becoming."

We call the next step "little," and it may be a small movement, or a silent, shared moment, or just saying in a plaintive voice, "You've gotten so Asian." But, it might also be an immense declaration. We call it the "next little step," but it's little in the same way an atom is little. It's a simple, tiny piece of just one element, but there's a ton going on in there. And it holds a massive amount of potential. Even though it's just the next thing, it could be *anything*. Screaming at the top of your lungs "I never want to see you again!" could be the next little thing, though that's also a pretty monstrous thing. It's the next little thing, the next logical thing, the next honest thing, the next reasonable thing, the next natural thing that might allow many possibilities to be revealed. As long as it's an authentic reaction to what has occurred and jibes with the reality created so far, we consider it a next little step.

> **As long as it's an authentic reaction to what has occurred and jibes with the reality created so far, we consider it a next little step.**

We talk about logic when considering the idea of improvising moment by moment. Given that we try to remain within the established reality at hand and in the scene thus far, we think simple logic is most sustainable. Large leaps of unclear thought will leave all of us unsure as to what's next. In the spirit of wanting to give people characters whom they can understand or relate to, we're not looking to develop characters who don't make sense or don't have a cause and effect. (It also would make your scene partners entirely unnecessary if they're not causing those effects. We feel our partner is the most vital person on the stage.) The sense of an understandable reality is more useful for making a sustainable relationship. Allowing ourselves to be affected in the most sensible, logical, and realistic way is easier than trying to manufacture a response that doesn't make any sense. And even if we find ourselves in an unreasonable world, we still can behave reasonably. Stay consistent with the logic that's been established. Even if it's some sort of Möbius strip logic, we can be that type of reasonable. No matter what show we're doing, we can always behave reasonably given these circumstances. When we're improvising one step at a time, we can be absurd—just not inconsistent.

Even though we're behaving logically, it doesn't mean we're improvising from our heads alone. TJ explains, "Ideally, in our show, I do something that makes David do something. David does something that makes me do something. Then I do something that makes David do something. If David says the line, 'We gotta sell some cars today,' he's going to say that in such a way that I am going to feel something from it. If he says it real high status, in a challenging way, then I'm going to know he means that *David* is going to sell some cars, and he's going to try to screw me out of a commission. If David says it with fear in his voice, I know we are together in this place, and we may be in trouble—that we had better sell some cars today, or the store is going under. The way David says that line will arouse something in me that I am not going to fight. The way his words are delivered inspires that feeling. Reading his voice and body language will stir something in me, and I'm going to believe it stirred the correct thing because it was the button that was pushed inside by what he did."

> **Allowing ourselves to be affected in the most sensible, logical and realistic way is an easier thing than trying to manufacture a response that doesn't make any sense.**

In some respects, we spend our whole show revealing a world in which it makes sense that one person says to another, "We gotta sell some cars today" or "You've gotten so Asian." Every step moves from that first moment. In going from one moment to the next, logic and true emotional reactions and honesty play a big role in the process.

We also trust that in taking the next little steps, we'll be fine without our great ideas. Those "great" ideas are the ones that usually lead us to drive a scene in a certain direction that we think would be really *wonderful* and *clever*. We wryly refer to those moments as our "great ideas" because, quite frankly, they always stink. We don't want to mess up a scene with what we think is going to be a great. Maybe it's a "great" laugh line; an "amazing" idea that would jolt the scene with a crazy plot twist; or an "awesome" way for the scene to end. They all prompt us to manipulate that scene into something it isn't. Those are our so-called "great" ideas. They are never good ideas.

We say, "All we can do is fuck up the show," because we believe the scene doesn't need our help. The scene doesn't need us to tell it where to go. The scene is just fine. We need to do the next natural thing in the situation at hand. Often, it isn't heroic or monumental or hilarious. It's just the next little thing. And we can't take that step without being absolutely present in the here and now. We have to be listening moment by moment; otherwise, how do we know to what we should react honestly?

If you're interested in this stuff, go ahead and try it. You'll change just by doing it, by getting onstage and trying it without interruption. Then try it some more. It's worth repeating: it's necessary to do this with people interested in heading in the same direction. Find some—and there may not be many—then make a deliberate effort to improvise in this fashion while trying to let go of any old, bad habits, such as making fear-based choices. But get on up and try it out. Do bad rehearsals. Perform dud shows. Then do it again. (At least that what we did.) The best teacher we've ever had is to DO IT over and over and over.

So here's a question: How do you get to the top of Mount Olympus?

You take every step in that direction.

IN CONVERSATION: *IMPROVISING ONE TINY STEP AT A TIME*

WITH DAVID

> Faith is not something to grasp, it is a state to grow into.
> — *Mahatma Gandhi*

PAM: "Behave reasonably and respond honestly in the moment" seems like an open proposition that ends at infinity.

DAVID: It does until it starts. Then infinity goes away real fast.

PAM: How do you avoid hemming and hawing? Or inventing?

DAVID: Trust that you are right about what you know. You don't have to invent if you pay attention.

PAM: At some point, David, you make an assumption. For example, you go from thinking you might be good buddies having a spat to realizing you're brothers at the end of a long family weekend. Guide me along the point when you know to trust that is the "correct" assumption.

DAVID: Having been observed as being true, it is correct. Doubt is of no use.

PAM: Yeah, but remember your poor students in the listening chapter exercise, the ones who you said couldn't move until they were compelled to move? Until that guy tied someone else's shoe, they made "incorrect" choices.

DAVID: Because they were frozen with doubt. They shouldn't do that. Don't do that.

PAM: David, if someone had started singing an operetta, you would have throttled him.

DAVID: Depends on why. (But yes.)

PAM: How can an improviser know when there is an impulse inside of him that is worthy of action?

DAVID: The honest and reasonable impulse is probably a good one. Trust the impulse.

You know how when you're doing a Harold and the scene is going on out there? You're on the back line and maybe it isn't going well, or maybe it's going very well but probably should end. Your body starts to move to edit the scene and end it, but you stop yourself for whatever reason. Maybe you're thinking, "I don't have anything to say to start a new scene," or "I don't want to step on their toes by ending their scene," or "I don't have anything clever to say." That first impulse, to edit, was correct. Your foot was right. Listen to your foot. I have to pay attention to my instincts. Just because I'm afraid is not a good enough reason not to proceed. There may be other reasons not to proceed, but merely being afraid is not reason enough.

PAM: Sometimes it's difficult to get past the blank mind of panic or the impulse to do *anything*, even if it's stupid. But I guess it comes down to trust. And faith, naturally. So if I focus on the moment at hand and the other person—which will shut off the noise of panic and self-doubt—I'll react with heart and honesty?

> **Listen to your foot.**

DAVID: Yes. The fear and worry also come from thinking about oneself ... that what I'm doing is not the right thing or is not enough, but that's not necessarily true. It's not to say that sitting there like a bump on a log all the time is the absolute right thing to do ... but it might be.

We worry that what we're doing is not enough; that we should be doing more, or we should be thinking more. All those things are wrong.

At our show at Town Hall in New York, there came to be a scene with a woman and some cops. Not all that much happened. Could have easily been ignored, thinking that not much came out of that. But TJ had us go back to some of the scene's characters a little later. Ordinarily, most people don't do that because they'd think it didn't bear fruit. But that's not what the show was saying. So we went back to find out what was going on. Turns out, it worked out pretty well.

PAM: By "that's not what the show was saying," do you mean you assumed you found yourself in that moment for a reason? You assumed it all was a good choice, the correct choice, and it was your job to discover why?

DAVID: Yes. It seemed like that was where it was heading, so we headed there. And it turns out plenty of stuff was going on. It's not a mistake unless you let it die. It may well be the groundwork for something that's coming later. Not everything has to be a home run.

PAM: Like when something bad happens to you, and it turns out to be the best thing that could have ever happened. Like getting fired, but then all these other opportunities open up for you.

DAVID: Right. Exactly. That scene didn't seem to be all that thrilling. Now I'm not going to go out and do a so-called fruitless scene on purpose, but that experience is applicable to a Harold or any show. You just never know what's going to be helpful.

PAM: We're just supposed to do the next little thing.

DAVID: Right. Which may be doing nothing—or very little. I think when people get paralyzed, they often sit there saying, "Uh ... uh ... " And the longer the time goes by, the more important it becomes. The longer I'm sitting there thinking, "Oh, this has to be a huge plot point," the worse it gets. That's just not helpful.

It's like when someone hands you a mimed birthday present, and you open it up. You look into an invisible object and try to determine what it is. And the longer you spend trying to figure out what it is, the more pressure you have on yourself to make it even better. And more time goes by ... and it has to be bigger. And more time goes by ... and it has to be more perfect. That's just a recipe for disaster.

Open the box. It's a hat. It's just tissue paper. Whatever the hell it is, it doesn't matter. The imaginary object in the imaginary box is not the scene. You and your stage partner are the scene.

IN CONVERSATION: *IMPROVISING ONE STEP AT A TIME*
WITH TJ

> Not only do we have to be good at waiting, we have to love
> it. Because waiting is not waiting, it is life ... I believe in the
> appreciation for simplicity, the everyday—the ability to dive deeply
> into the banal and discover life's hidden richness—is where success,
> let alone happiness, emerges.
> — *Josh Waitzkin, The Art of Learning*

PAM: There is a common reaction to improvisers first hearing your "next little step" approach. They say it works for you and David because you're supremely talented improvisers, but worry that, in the hands of beginning or developing improvisers, the audience would be bored out of their skulls.

TJ: Dave and I have done workshops with absolute beginners and had them sit down, listen to each other, and respond honestly. There were compelling, beautiful scenes that were way more logical than most of the scenes that you'd see from people who've been doing it for ten years. So I think it's more universally applicable than people might imagine.

And it takes practice. If you try it and it doesn't work, because you're just staring at the clock for a while, you get scared of trying it again. Like anything else, chances are if you want to get halfway decent at something, you're going to suck at it for a while.

PAM: Do you remember the moment when you got the idea that this approach was the path you wanted to take?

TJ: I don't remember the exact time, but I can recall scenes where I was trying to push too hard. I remember doing a scene where I was breeding chickens, and for some reason, I had named them all after popes. It was one of the first shows I did at iO, and I was just working so damn hard! There I was, trying to come up with fifteen pope names, but unfortunately, I didn't remember a single thing about my scene partner, who they were, what they were doing, where they were, what they had said.

Now I think about scenes differently. I might remember them as something my scene partner did, or, for example, as "the one between the two ex-lovers who are now both newly married."

PAM: You think of scenes in terms of relationships instead of details?

TJ: Yeah, I think of them in terms of two people as opposed to the comedic premise of the scene.

PAM: If we're taking things step by step, it seems we need to speak and act upon the emotional feeling in the room between the two people.

TJ: There is this exercise I call "The Johnson File." You get five or six people up. These are a series of two-person scenes with one person onstage and the other person making an entrance. And the players rotate through, doing five or six two-person scenes all in sequence and taking turns as the person starting onstage. Each scene has the same exact relationship, and each scene has the same exact first line.

For example, they are roommates, and the entering person is going to state the first line, "Great party last night." The improvisers' job is to decide what happened last night that would make them come into the room the way they do and make the line come out of their mouths the way it does. Maybe they hooked up with the most gorgeous person of their dreams, or they woke up to find someone had crapped in their pillowcase. Or the TV was gone. So they would walk in and say, "Great party last night," in a specific emotional way.

It shouldn't be a guessing game, so you don't want that second line to be a guess why the other person felt that way. When I do that exercise, I want them to engage in how last night impacted that kitchen, that morning, at that moment.

PAM: And how it made them feel.

TJ: Yeah, to engage their current emotion as opposed to the unseen event in the past. Like if your character is sad, my first impulse in that moment probably shouldn't be to guess why you are sad, but instead to focus on what do I *do* when you are sad? Do I come to you? Do I ignore you? Are you always sad and it drives me crazy? Are you never sad, so this is emergency mode? Do you eat when you're sad? If so, then I'll start making eggs. Engage the present moment that this emotion brings out. So rather even than saying, "Oh, you're sad," I just can start making the eggs.

PAM: So, nearly three-quarters of the way through a *TJ & Dave* show, when the story seems to be forming, are you not thinking any moves ahead? Are you starting to connect some dots?

TJ: No, we're trying to figure out what might be the most interesting moment to explore, which couple of people have the most going on between them. If we start a show with two people in a restaurant but realize there is way more interesting stuff going on between the waiter and the chef, we're going to want to go to the waiter and the chef. We try to find the warmest water to get into.

PAM: Is that just who you and Dave find interesting?

TJ: It's who *people* find interesting. Do you want watch two people who are bored with each other, or do you want to watch two people who excite or infuriate each other?

For example, we start with two people in a restaurant, but we find out that the chef and the waiter have way more in common, so we stay in that kitchen scene. Accidentally, because that kitchen scene was intriguing or exciting to us, we're going to spend a while on that scene. At some point, we're bound to realize, "Oh, dammit. We should have gone out to check on that table again." So we go back out, and those people were waiting for their food. And this delayed meal is another crummy thing that happened to them that night—and on their *anniversary*. Now it seems like the story is the two people who had a horrible tenth anniversary. That may read as a narrative, but it's an accidental by-product of the fact that we were exploring relationships that interested us. Does that make sense?

PAM: Yes. It seems like quite a challenge for improvisers to hold all that in their heads, especially when they're playing all the characters. I don't know how you guys do it.

TJ: I think it's so much easier because we are the guys who have done everything. We've been in the relationship. We've been the two people at the table. We've been the waiter and the cook. And, hell, all that is taking place in twenty minutes. If you can't rely on your brain to remember what *you just did* for the last twenty minutes, then you've got larger world problems to worry about. You may not be able to take care of yourself. You might not be able to feed yourself if that's the case.

PAM: True. But you're talking and thinking at the same time!

TJ: Ideally. But the hope is that you're thinking whenever you're speaking! These reactions are drawn out of you, but they're not without thought. There is a lot of paying attention. There is a lot of listening.

PAM: While you're playing the chef and the waiter, are you still thinking about those other two people waiting in the restaurant and what that experience is like for them?

TJ: I think more often than not, one of us suddenly realizes, "Oh, damn. We forgot about those people. I wonder what they've been doing this whole time?" And if we go back to them, we pick them up already in progress with the logical explanation of what happened in the last fifteen minutes that we haven't seen them.

This shift is predicated on the assumption that they weren't having a good time in the first place. Otherwise, Dave and I would have stayed on them instead of going to the chef and the waiter. If they weren't having a good time earlier, we can assume that it has gotten a little bit worse, exacerbated by the fact that their appetizer has not come out and nobody has come out to fill their water glasses or bring the bread basket.

PAM: There always seems to be agreement with those transitions in your show. Obviously, you don't know what the next scene is going to be, for example, when you move from the restaurant patrons to the waiter and chef. Often, you automatically seem to know where the new scene is taking place and exactly who you are. That is where I find some of the magic.

TJ: We don't exactly know. We pay attention to what's going on and make logical assumptions. Chances are that unless they walked in as soon as the restaurant opened, these aren't the only two people in there. We might fill out the restaurant a little with another couple sitting at another table. So if I see Dave in a chair in a place where we didn't establish that first table, I can probably assume that he's a diner at a different table. Because we don't make huge, illogical jumps, there is a good chance Dave is going to play a character who has been mentioned or implied or could be assumed to be there.

And chances are, he won't be in a place that hasn't been named, described, or talked about. If the only described or talked about places are the dining room and the kitchen, he's probably going to be in that dining room. And he wasn't sitting where the only other two known people were dining, so he's more than likely going to be yet another diner. If I haven't already walked out of that back room as a waiter, then I'm probably going to be eating with him. Or, if it's not illogical to assume there is another waiter on shift, maybe I'll be another waiter. Depending on what the cook and the waiter talked about, if it was love issues, maybe I'm a pretty good-looking waitress, and that was the nature of what got them in such a heated talk. Maybe one of them had a boner for this lady.

Deconstructing in this way makes it sound very complicated. But in actuality it's not, because any one of those moves will be fine.

PAM: I think it's remarkably simple and elegant. We see these moments of magic that look like you're reading each other's minds because you've limited the amount of jumps you can make, right?

TJ: We're not suddenly going to be on a deserted island. We're not going to be in the middle of a transatlantic flight. If the show ever gives the impression of it being telepathic or magical, it's really not. If it is a trick, it's the simplest trick that's ever been done.

PAM: Okay, that's not true, but I'll let you get away with it.

TJ: But it is. As you said, it's simple. It's not complicated. It's just a right triangle. It's simply pretty, but it's not elaborate or clever.

PAM: I can see how this step-by-step approach allows you to live in the neighborhood where magic is more likely to occur.

TJ: It makes us more likely to be on the same page because there are only a certain number of options out there. It seems hard because every moment allows an infinite number of possibilities. But any one of those choices, made with integrity and commitment to the choice you made, will all work. So even though there are infinite possibilities, it's utterly simple in that any honest step in any one of those directions will work.

PAM: How do you access or develop that sweet spot in your heart to better react honestly in the moment? I'm not looking for theory or philosophy here. I want to know what practical steps I can take to improve this skill.

TJ: Apply life. I think I got a lot better when I turned thirty. As I've gotten older, I understand a little bit better than I did when I was twenty or twenty-five. And then I apply life to rehearsal.

A lot of people say they don't care for rehearsal, or they want that vibe of the live audience. But you never have a safer place than when you're in rehearsal with your team. That should be when you try everything. That's truly your workshop. I don't mean to be cheeky with it, but get older, pay attention, keep living. And then bring that experience with you.

PART FOUR

INHABITING SPACE

15

THE PEOPLE WE PLAY

Acting is memorization. Improvisation is living.
— *David Shepherd*

You are what you do, not what you say you'll do.
— *C.G. Jung*

TJ and David's approach to character development and relationship incorporates many previously discussed topics. Included are paying attention, the importance of one's stage partner, grounded scene work, experiencing discovery and, especially, their goal of behaving with honesty. Even though TJ and David will say they play characters very much like themselves, one sees a wide range of interesting, nuanced, multi-dimensional characters at a *TJ & Dave* show. Quite often, the audience feels like they recognize these people. A World War II veteran might remind someone of their grandfather. A lazy but well-meaning brother may resemble a friend. And we've all worked with numbskulls.

TJ AND DAVID ON PEOPLE THEY PLAY

When it comes to characters in *TJ & Dave*, we tend to play pretty close to ourselves. David plays people who look, sound, and act similar to him. Likewise, TJ's characters often resemble TJ, though he might play a young gal hot for a night on the town, an older gentleman waking up from a nap or a little boy shopping for licorice on his birthday. We often play ourselves with a slight exaggeration in a certain direction. They're us as other people. Sometimes the characters become more specific and defined. Sometimes we're playing screaming Germans. But it's still us in there.

Del Close taught David to wear his characters "as a thin veil," meaning that it's not necessary for the actor to disappear completely under his character when improvising. We take this to mean we're not hiding behind a character. We are in charge. In *TJ & Dave*, one of us may be playing a forgetful mother character, but you can see us under there. We're not fooling anybody into believing we've suddenly become a 64-year-old, hard of hearing, church-going mom.

We take this "thin veil" approach to character development for a variety of reasons. For one, we play ourselves best. Neither of us melts into our characters while improvising. When we wear our characters lightly, we're playing to our strengths. We don't have the abilities or prosthetics to pull off several generations of a madcap family. We don't have a stable of fully developed, big characters we can pull out in a show when it suits us. We seldom play broad characters. We also don't play archetypes or people we know. That's not the type of actors we are at this point. And, conveniently, we don't find it helpful for the way we improvise in *TJ & Dave*.

That's not what the scene is about. It's not a scene of archetypes. The scene is a particular guy in a particular setting—he's a real guy. We may or may not play him very well, but he's not the archetypical "father-in-law." Since we are fully improvising, we play only the people who exist in a specific situation in the here and now.

We're not saying it's bad to play broad characters, but that style doesn't jibe with our approach to improvisation. If we were playing in another form outside our show, our approach to characters might be different. For instance, we could play in a show where the goal is to be funny. If it requires, we might play a goofy character, someone to walk in, deliver a joke or be a foil, and then leave. That works for a blackout or a short scene. But it doesn't work for us in our show, which needs to be sustained for an hour and where our goal is to be real rather than funny. When it comes to characters, especially main characters, we find it easier to come from a simple, familiar, honest place.

We play real people in *TJ & Dave* because it works best to behave as if the people are real. If we were busy "acting," then we would not be honestly responding in the moment. That's why we perform as if we are stepping into the shoes of people who were living their lives before we took the stage and will continue to do so after the lights go down. If we played characters or caricatures or people we know, we would be limited by those set, stock personalities or our impersonations of them, and that would impede the act of discovery for us. So we perform as if—and indeed believe—we are temporarily inhabiting the lives of real people who make their own decisions and speak their own thoughts. These people are previously unknown to us but certainly not imaginary. They are so real that often after a show, we might say to each other, "I can't believe what an asshole that guy was," referring to a character we just played.

One day, a friend asked David how the previous night's show went. "Fine, it got a little dark," he replied. "This one poor guy ended up killing himself." The friend asked incredulously, "You do realize that's you, don't you?"

It is us, but it isn't, and it's difficult to put this dynamic into words. We're both participating in the lives of the characters while, at the same time, we're observers. But we don't need to understand it or put it into words. We only need to start the show with a blank slate. Any preconceived notion would defeat our purpose of discovering whose lives we are inhabiting. We are not inventing the characters; they are revealing themselves to us over the course of the show.

> **The character reveals itself through playing the relationship.**

When it comes to characters, we are primarily interested in exploring their roles in the scenic relationships. And that's where our main focus is: the relationship. We're trying to experience their interaction on as many levels as we can. The character reveals itself through playing the relationship. The way we see it, relationship and character support each other. The character might inform the relationship, the relationship will bring things out of the character, so they fuel each other. When we go into a show, we're not going in there with the specific goal that we need to serve a relationship or a character. We're just looking to serve the show.

We approach improvisation as a constant examination of the moment. So when a performer is asking, "Who am I? Who am I? Who am I?" we find that to be an unnecessarily self-centered and less useful focus. Ultimately we find more value in gently asking ourselves, "What is happening? What is already happening here?" We're not referring to an activity that is happening. We are reminding ourselves that the show is not just about ourselves and our characters; *it's about the dynamic between us.* An even better question is, "What is this that we're in right now?" By this type of examination, we attempt to engage in a less selfish and more cooperative approach.

In one show, David played a real Johnny-on-the-spot spa attendant eager to take care of a pair of guys who were there to unwind (one of whom was also played by David). A couple of times, TJ's character mentioned wishing there was a garbage can or fresh pineapple in their room. The attendant quickly bent over backwards to provide those things in a way that was so gushing it seemed to have romantic intent. If we had only asked, "Who am I?," if David were overly focused either on the character-y aspects of his guy or the functionality of his attendant role, or if TJ were only concerned with his character's desire to unwind or for fresh fruit, we might have missed what was really happening between the two people. Because what was really going on—and what was most important in that scene—was a spa attendant's assiduous attempt to connect with someone, anyone, in the world. There was a man who chose a career in service as a way to put himself in an arena in which he could be someone for somebody. And there was a spa-goer being torn, in the light of a kind offering, between rejoining a more comfortable conversation with his friend and attempting to not damage a clearly tender soul. When we focus solely on our character or function, we tend to miss the moments to discover "What is this that we're in right now?" These moments are brought about simultaneously and cooperatively between two improvisers who are paying attention to one another. We're not individually creating our characters; rather we're both noticing them together in the evolving relationships being slowly revealed onstage as we ask, "What is this that we're in right now?"

When it comes to character development, our stage partners tell us and the audience all we need to know. The information we learn from them is more than just facts. We're looking for the way they treat us. If it's casual in nature, that's helpful because then we may experience we have a camaraderie. If it's formal or antagonistic, we learn something from that as well. Regardless of the words they use, it's how our stage partners are behaving that most informs our character.

> **We approach improvisation as a constant examination of the moment before us.**

David remembers Del Close saying that the job isn't to be a scary person; the job is for the other people to be scared. If a boss character is frightened of her secretary, then it becomes clearer to the improviser playing the secretary that she is frightening, or at least a person who the boss character finds scary. That character does not need to become frightening. She already is scary. All we have to do is keep playing her exactly the same way as we have all along. We do not need to immediately do more. We merely notice and continue to be, slowly evolving at a real human pace. To do otherwise would be a lie that negates the previously established reality.

> **When it comes to character development, our stage partners tell us and the audience all we need to know.**

One of us could play the most lovely woman in the world, and she's maimed and clumsily falling all over herself and cruel. All that's going to matter is that everyone who sees her thinks she's the most lovely woman in the world. That character is informed by how everyone else sees her. And then even if the most truly lovely woman in the world walked into the show, if we played it real casual, then she ceases to be the most lovely woman in the world.

Though this approach involves some letting go of control and trusting in our scene partner to make our character real, we can reassure ourselves that we're going to take care of each other. When it comes down to it, it's not necessarily faith in each other; it's a belief that we're going to take care of each other. And so far, neither of us has ever been sold out by one other. (We have sold ourselves out plenty.)

We help each other realize who we are. And at the beginning of the show, we quite simply haven't learned enough about ourselves from our stage partners yet, which is another reason we wear our characters lightly and realistically. At the top of a show, we don't have enough information to play even a semi-formed character. Otherwise, it would be fabricated. As we know more—and, sometimes it happens pretty quickly—our characters may become more clearly defined and detailed.

> **Rather than inventing characters out of thin air, we simply must pay attention acutely to discover the character we are already.**

This point seems to be the fundamental difference in the way we talk about improvisation compared to how we hear others talk about it. We truly believe that we are discovering what's already going on. We're not making it up. It works the same way in life. When you meet someone for the first time, you can't know everything about them. A person's character is revealed little by little as you get to know them. And it may change as you learn more facts and have more experiences together. When he ends up saving your ass on some make-or-break year-end project, that guy at the office, whom you hated at first, may turn out to be not so bad after all.

As you probably already guessed, Heat and Weight guide our approach to character as well. We examine each other, our selves, and the moment between us. Small facial expressions, body stance, proximity, that certain something behind the eyes—it all informs us as to who we are as characters and our relationship to one another. If we had come onstage with a character in mind, we might think we know exactly who we are and what's going on in the scene before the lights even come up. But then we'd meet each other's eyes and realize none of that makes sense given what's already going on and what we're receiving from each other. We wouldn't be following the show as it exists already. We wouldn't be behaving and responding honestly in the moment. So, instead, we come on playing only the characters who are already there onstage when the lights come up.

Our usual *tabula rasa* mindset changes a bit for characters introduced later in the show because they must fit in the established reality. So logical reasoning, previous information, and circumstance may dictate the type of characters we play as the show proceeds. If someone is mentioned, we integrate that information into the character, because it is now fact. In one show, it was revealed that an elderly father was upstairs taking a nap. From the conversation between his wife and her adult son, before we even met the man, we discovered approximately how old he was and that he was hard of hearing. We learned he was fairly religious. Since we're already playing his wife and son, that information colored his character too: he was the type of guy who would have married the mother character and been a father to that son. The established reality of the scene shaped this man before he revealed himself, and we had to recognize and reflect those facts in our portrayal of that character.

TJ explains the father character this way: "We knew this guy was in the war, so he was older. We knew David was his kid. Especially when improvising, if David flinches from me at some point, I'm allowed to know that my character is tough. So I might start holding my shoulders differently because I'm well acquainted with being able to swing a fist pretty well. And thankfully, being improvisation, I don't have to have that body or mind entirely formed, as with film or a play. We're allowed to let that character evolve. That character is going to look and speak somewhat differently after eighteen minutes into the show than at the three-minute mark. The interaction with David is going to allow me to know more about this person I'm playing." From the start of the show, there is a factual and an emotional biography that's being created for each character. So we try to remind ourselves to be true to all the things we've said about that person up to that point.

Reality and logic determine character.

In addition to previously discovered personal information, location and timing may end up informing a character as well. In another show, David's character found himself stomping on his cellphone at a bus station. It felt like there would be other people around. After all, when was the last time you were in a perfectly empty bus station? At that point, the discovery of those other characters became dictated by the logical reasoning of the folks most likely found at a bus station. TJ found himself playing a nosey foreign man who says to David's phone-stomping character, "Dude, what up? Why, dude?" After that interaction, it occurred to us that, logically, TJ's foreign guy would have a traveling companion. And, mostly likely, he would also have an accent. So David eventually appeared as the friend, who had been sitting next to TJ's foreign character, working a Sudoku puzzle the whole time. The fact that he was immersed in a puzzle sensibly explains why we didn't hear from him earlier in the interaction. In those cases, we do not begin with a totally blank slate because we must allow the agreed upon, established reality to inform those characters. Logic guides all, including character and relationship.

When we step into new characters, we change our voices or posture, which helps communicate to each other and the audience that we're playing a different person. We change our voices to fit the characters. For example, someone who was in World War Two is older, and age wears on their vocal chords. That character sounds and holds their body differently than someone who is fresh out of college. Again, reality and logic determine character.

We need to trust that this information about our characters and their relationships can be conveyed without stating it explicitly, but by behaving that way. We could choose to make sure we're border collie-ing everything here and over-state the characters' relationships to each other. Or we could think—*trust*—that our partner will get it. We aim towards the latter. We trust that our stage partner is on the same page as we are.

In the process of gleaning information about our character, we try to be subtle about receiving it. Most of what we're learning is new information for the improviser, but it's not new to the character. So if there's the feeling that our character makes the meals in the house, we'll be a lot handier or looser in the kitchen and with knives than we would have been up to that point. Now there is more information at hand. Even though we improvisers may have just discovered this character is facile at dicing and slicing, we need to present that as ordinary and unsurprising because there is nothing new under the sun (or in the kitchen) to his character.

It's also a circular thing. For instance, say TJ was playing a cook. He might have gotten the feeling that his character was handy in the kitchen from noticing some small thing David did or said, which intimated TJ's character had spent a long time peeling potatoes. And that was probably in response to an observation or feeling David picked up about TJ's character. We continually learn from what we've seen and inform each other as to who we are and how we feel about each other, but we can't portray it like it's sudden information. If it's not done somewhat subtly, then it looks like this 70-year-old man just found out he's good in the kitchen. The truth is, he's known that he was handy around vegetables since he had to cut potatoes at age nineteen at his grandma's country restaurant. So when we pay very close attention and assume what we're learning is fact, we can ease into our characters in a, hopefully, more confident and graceful fashion.

SHOW, DON'T TELL: EXPLORING RELATIONSHIPS THROUGH BEHAVIOR

As mentioned earlier, one of the common rules of improvisation is "Show, don't tell," which encourages the actor to choose an action over just talking about it. We apply the principle behind "Show, don't tell" to relationship and character development as well. Instead of talking about our relationship, we try to explore the relationship through our modes of behavior, the tones of our voices, our body language, through *relating* to one another. Some folks try to be overly helpful to their scene partners by calling out the premise of the scene and stating the subtext straight out. At the top of the show, they'll say things like, "You're a bad brother, and you're always leaving." Sometimes improvisers become overly specific and expositional when discovering their characters, which tends, in our view, to yield a less elegant scene. Instead, while outwardly we might be playing two brothers talking about our childhood memories, we are really communicating with each other about the nature of our fraternal dynamic. We don't have to hear one brother say to the other, "Get off your ass. You're always slacking off, and I'm fed up" in order to discover that there is some tension and resentment between these two guys as they recall a family trip to Yellowstone.

We don't often speak explicitly to the nature of the characters' relationships. We rarely find ourselves in scenes that turn into encounter sessions or heart-to-hearts about the characters' relationships. We don't often do that when we're offstage, so why would we do it onstage? When was the last time you talked to your best buddy about your friendship together? Or to your dad about your relationship? Or to your boss about your work dynamic together? Unless you're in the early heat of a romance or a crisis point of some sort, those types of intense conversations seldom happen in actual life. As we're exploring our characters, we're trying to make everything understood with as little expositional communication as possible. Sometimes it works. Other times, not so much. But that's where we're aiming.

When we do explicitly state the nature of a relationship between two people, we try to do it when it comes naturally and isn't born of fear or doubt that our stage partner isn't with us. TJ says, "I would say that we might get to the point where one of us might say to the other, 'You're an irresponsible idiot.' But that would be because those words felt right at the time. It wasn't because David didn't know that his character was an irresponsible idiot. It was because my character's frustration level would have driven me to want to say that out loud, so his goddamn ears had to wrassle with it. So I can sometimes state exactly what's going on, but not out of doubt that David or the audience doesn't already know that fact. Instead, I might say it explicitly, so David's character has to swallow it. I would say it at a moment that is more scene-appropriate and character-appropriate." As such, we try to make sure that our words are coming out of the character's mouth, not out of the improviser's mouth.

> **We're supposed to be responding honestly in the particular moment. That's it. That's the end of our responsibility.**

It goes back to the erroneous belief that you're supposed to be "funny," or to be doing something. No. We're supposed to be responding honestly in the particular moment. That's it. That's the end of our responsibility. In fact, to do anything more than that will fuck it up. We trust that what we have right now is already fascinating. It's already a ton of information. We don't need to report more. Throughout the course of a show, we learn plenty that never gets mentioned. If it needs mentioning or it factors in, it will be. But we get tons of information that we are both aware of but that never makes it to the audience.

In our effort to discover the characters gradually being revealed to us onstage, we tend to play fairly regular people. When we're reacting honestly and logically in a show, big, dramatic characters tend to stick out like sore thumbs, just as they do most of the time in real life. So, we don't often feel called upon to play kooky people. Overall, we find it works best when the show is centered around a grounded character because an oddball or unintelligent character, for example, isn't enough to hold down a show. Just as a jokey scene won't provide a solid base for a one-hour show, a one-dimensional, broad character won't support us, or the show, very long, either. There isn't enough genuineness there. So we try to play everyone, especially our central characters, from a solid and honest place.

Sometimes, we do run into kooky people. Since we're being guided by the show, now and then a weird or wacky or truly dense human ends up living in that world. We may be called upon to play, for instance, a screaming Italian family in a backed up kitchen, but those tend not to be our main characters. But sometimes when we're in a grounded, stable show—and the moment organically arises—we'll find ourselves playing a silly character or two.

Even when these more extreme people enter our world, they must still be played with the same multi-dimensionality as anyone else. Here we can apply the idea of "developing" (as opposed to heightening) as we explore these characters in all directions. People are more than their traits. The previously mentioned spa attendant was more than a super-efficient functionary. A stupid person is more than just a stupid person. We can't afford to play completely stupid people onstage because we're not good enough actors to fool an audience into thinking we don't know something that we actually do know. (Not that we aren't stupid. Just that we're not good enough to play even stupider.) As a result, we wouldn't look like we're playing a dingdong; rather, we'd come off as liars. If we're searching for honesty, that tactic will render only disastrous results.

So when we play characters, we must try to play them fully and not just their wacky aspects. Second City founder, Bernie Sahlins, used to point out the distinction between playing a character and playing *at* a character. In playing at a character, there is always a separation where the actor (or improviser) is apart from the person he or she is playing. It's like looking at the audience with a wink, saying, "Wouldn't it be funny if I were this stupid? But we all know I'm not. I am much cooler than this geek I'm playing." In *TJ & Dave*, we try to play the characters, or ideally, the humans.

Sometimes those humans are not the sharpest bulbs in the drawer. Or sometimes we're called upon to play children. How do we still play these characters to the top of our intelligence? The answer is: we try to play them as their whole selves. Kids, for instance, are often astoundingly intelligent. David recalls one of his sons' friends who knew more about European history since the fourth grade than David ever will. Another kid in the second grade knew all about Pangea and every epoch, geologic period, and dinosaur. "Kids are really smart about facts sometimes ... and for sure they are smart about observations."

Even though children's experiences are limited by their shorter time on earth, we cannot play to those limitations. It isn't helpful to our scene partners if we only play them as one-dimensional characters or uninformed people. It may be self-preservation, but even when the scene calls for us to play a sexist jerk, we will sooner or later try to find some decent quality or redemptive value in that multi-faceted person. So if that jerk character is going on and on about his misadventures with a stripper in Vegas, we figure that only some level of insecurity would make someone talk like that. He has that layer, which is not entirely unsympathetic, but he's also clearly insecure and so he needs to build himself up with his bravado. It's our job to present all his layers, including those vulnerabilities. Even though we are playing that sexist jerk, and he is definitely an idiot, we might play him as insightful. We may be called upon to portray that he, in his dimwittedness, may be able to see something that the "smarter" characters couldn't. (Notice we use "may" a lot. We try to remain open to change based on the moments we are experiencing.)

Ultimately, we're trying to give people every reason to believe that what's going on is real, even though it's not. We want to give the audience every reason to believe that the people we play are real in their world. As with object work, if we take a half-second to see this coffee cup as real, then it becomes more real. Similarly, if we take a half-second to notice a person, then we might be able to feel them and see them as real. Then, as information is added, we can start to dress the mannequin, rather than tossing clothes at something more ethereal. If we can get a better picture of these people we're playing in our heads, we have a better shot at portraying them more believably.

Let's say we are playing a hardware store manager, previously described as a persnickety, Type A personality. We have some information then as to how we would portray that body and how that person would deal with an environment. He might be the kind of guy who looks at the nail bin with the mind to count how many nails are in there. So, he's going to move differently and focus on other things than the kid who is off smoking half a joint on his break.

It may look as though there is a bit of magical chemistry between us. But we think that the primary skills of paying attention and subtly using what's been learned (with a bit of sleight of hand) are entirely learnable skills that anyone can apply to their improvisation and character work. It's like playing bridge. In the beginning, the bidding is in front of everyone, and you tell your partner what you have in your hand. Everybody is privy to it. Like in our show, everyone is privy to everything we communicate to one another. We just happen to be listening a little differently.

> **Everyone is privy to everything we communicate to one another. We just happen to be listening a little differently.**

David tells this story:

We were doing a show with Tracy Letts, who performs with us now and then, and at one point, Tracy said, 'You know that guy? So-and-so's kid?' In unison, TJ and I said, 'Derrick?' The crowd was kind of stunned, not knowing how we could possibly have decided to name that character the same name independently. It must have looked like telepathy. But all we did was remember that he was named earlier. We just paid attention. All we did was listen when someone called him Derrick—they said it quietly, so, clearly, not everyone heard it.

We truly believe a lot of what we do is paying attention—absorbing all of it, including intangibles, such as how our stage partner's behavior is making us feel. If TJ finds himself feeling delighted by something David is doing, even though objectively he has no reasonable proof to be delighted, he's going to play that nonetheless. And while we're paying attention, we're also participating in the scene. Sure, it takes a bit of juggling to do both of these things at the same time, but it's worth a shot if you're interested in giving it a try.

As you may have gleaned by now, we're not intentionally developing character and relationship as much as we're intensely observing. We want to put ourselves in a position to realize who our characters are and what is their relationship to one another. Realization being the cool idea here: The key to realizing who we are quite simply is paying attention right now ... and then taking the next little step.

After all this thought about characters in improvisation, we'd like to propose that improvisers stop calling them "characters" in the first place. Often, if you set out to play a character, you actually end up defining him/her by their physical characteristics or traits, such as a limp. How about we start calling them "people"? Instead of hearing someone say, "I played this great character last night," we'd love to hear, "I played this great *person* last night." Maybe if we thought of playing people instead of characters, we might bring a more fully fleshed-out person to the scene—complete with their point of view, who they are or who they might become. And in our experience, that's a much richer, deeper well to from which to draw.

IN CONVERSATION: *PLAYING MULTIPLE CHARACTERS*

In *TJ & Dave*, many characters may be revealed over the course of the show, and they're all played by TJ or David. Quite often, a single character is played by both of them as they each move in and out of the characters as need demands. The duo is so skilled at embodying several different multi-dimensional characters within a single scene that often, when recalling one of their shows, it may seem like there was a whole cast of actors. It can be a bit mind-boggling. Memories of whole families, restaurant staff, and double dates were really just two plainly dressed men sitting on bentwood chairs. Here, we'll focus on TJ and David's ability to play several characters in the same show. Let's try to break down the skills they use, both those applied deliberately and those that come about more naturally over the course of the show.

PAM: In the process of playing characters, is there any part that feels conscious to you at this point?

TJ: For me, the physicality of a character is more conscious. If I very much want this person to be perceived as a tall, lanky, elegant woman, conscious thought is involved for me to do what needs to be done body-wise in order to best convey that impression.

PAM: Those technical matters are more conscious for you then?

TJ: Yes, the mental effort of trying to climb into a mind that doesn't necessarily behave as mine might operate on more semi-conscious levels. But other aspects are definitely conscious in trying to complete the total portrayal of a character.

PAM: I feel most uncomfortably self-conscious when I'm playing a character that I have absolutely no experience with, say, a migrant farm worker.

DAVID: I think the only time you might end up with characters you can't play, is when there's too much fact and story. Like when we play surgeons. Neither one of us has ever performed surgery or been conscious when it's performed on us. We can still play surgeons, just not good ones. Your migrant worker as a father who is trying to do the best he can for his family, I can understand. I can imagine what it's like to bend over for twelve hours too, but again, it's the *relationship*. I'm a father. It's not that label of "migrant worker." It's who I am to these other people.

PAM: The fluidity at which you play multiple characters in the same show often astounds me. Have there been muscles you've strengthened or tricks you've discovered that helped it become easier for you to keep track of which character you're playing?

DAVID: I have a pretty good trick ... super secret one ... it seems to work better when you pay very close attention.

There is a story of a theater director in England who would come in half an hour before the show and tell the person who played the duke the night before, "Today you're the butler ..." And he would change the whole casting around. So they had better have been paying attention to blocking and everything because they're going to have to play all the roles. It's the same thing with us. I'd better be paying attention to TJ because I may have to be that person. Really, that is the trick.

Physicalization is also very helpful for the clarity of characters. A recent show took place entirely in the seats of a movie theater, so it was difficult. At one point, TJ put his foot up on the chair in front. (Actually, he moved his foot up into space, suggesting that he'd put his foot on the chair in front.) Twenty-five minutes later, I put my foot up similarly, and the whole audience knew immediately what was going on. So it's very helpful to make physical distinctions between characters. And it's not just for the audience. It's for everybody. It's for you and your fellow players.

PAM: You give yourself a little hook to hang your thin veil on, I guess.

TJ: As far as playing multiple characters, the hardest part is jumping back into their mental process, their mindset, and how their thoughts and emotions motivate their actions. The easier part is thinking, "Yeah, this is the guy with shoulders up to his ears." If the physicality can help me get back into their mindset, then that's the really useful part of playing multiple characters.

DAVID: It can be something simple, like the way you hold your hand or a guy who always has a can of soda in hand or is smoking. Whatever it happens to be, it's helpful to have a little something for everyone involved—to tell TJ, to inform the audience, and to remind myself of who this is.

TJ: In some ways, it's the substitute for that one little scarf or a pair of glasses that you'd have in a scripted play. We don't have access to that in improvisation, so for ease of the people who didn't get the program before, we use a little physicality of some sort.

To be clear, a character is a different mind, and that's my way to remember what their body is like. The way someone's mind works, their emotional states, and how they view the world, will eventually inform their bodies. People terrified of the world hold their bodies like they're terrified of the world. Maybe that's why it's useful to me that someone who is uptight and always looking for problems is going to lead with his nose or have his shoulders up by his neck. Ideally, their physicality is attached to their point of view. So if I can use this physicality like the back door into their mind, then that's of practical use to me. The character Chill Phil was called Chill Phil because he looked chill. If I have to play that character of David's, maybe I can get into that relaxed body, the shoulders that were way back, the loose knees. Then maybe I have a shot at getting to that point of view and his mind. Even if I do everything physically right but can't get hold of how that player thinks, then I'm going to be useless. Because I'm not going to react in the way that is the true basis of that character, regardless of whether I get that voice and body right.

PAM: So if you could only do one of those skills, it's more important to find their point of view?

TJ: ... get their mind.

PAM: I want to take a moment to talk about transitions between multiple characters because there are times when it looks completely seamless to me. In one show I saw, there was a moment at the end that just killed me. The scene was a phone call between two women. David just uncrossed his legs, shifted the angle he was sitting at, and suddenly he was doing a scene between three goofballs who worked at the office. That looked like magic to me. Can you break it down?

TJ: My guess is that David sat like that character in the same general place on the stage, and we both felt an edit point.

DAVID: Also, if I sat in that way, it may have been the distinguishing characteristic of that person, which would have been known by TJ. So no matter what he's doing, when TJ sees me do that, he knows I'm that other person and, since we're not working in a time jump, we must be in a different place.

TJ: David doesn't do anything without a reason. So I know if that happened, he's not the same character he just was. If it looks like something about the reality might have been destroyed or it looks like he walked through a wall (I know Dave doesn't ever do that), then I know that it's a different scene purely by logistics. There might have been something said in that previous scene that indicated to both of us that it might be a good idea to go see those other people now.

PAM: Do you indicate a change of scene by moving the chairs as shorthand to communicate to each other and the audience?

TJ: That's one thing that could happen. But it could be the pace at which one of us moves. Usually, if we're indicating a change of scene, there could be a long, slow cross. Or it could be that it doesn't seem like that character would quickly walk stage left, so that could indicate a change. Sometimes, Dave could be assuming another character within that current location. We don't have any set shorthand. I think both of us feel like, "Huh. That felt a little different ... something is happening here, whatever that is."

PAM: Would you agree, David?

DAVID: Yes. It's just paying attention. "Oh, this is not the same guy. TJ's moving at a pace uncharacteristic for the person he was playing, so he must be someone else." I wouldn't have noticed that change unless I know how that first person behaves. If I don't know who he is, I won't know he's different. I have to know who he is first.

TJ: There might be a break of eye contact as well. It's like saying, "Don't engage me right now. I'm not here. I'm not looking at you ... okay, now I'm here." And if you're not paying attention, you won't realize that we're not looking at each other.

PAM: You're always assuming and trusting the other person is right, doing the right thing at the right moment.

DAVID: Because they are. There is a bit of magic to it as well. And there is no explanation for it. It may only be that we're both confident that the other person is paying attention. That is the crux of it. But I do have this thing with TJ that is beyond explanation in how we somehow seem to be able to communicate in a way that doesn't always make a lot of sense.

PAM: What is the thinking that goes into staying with a character or switching to another character? TJ, you mentioned before that there are natural edit points that sometimes indicate a time to switch.

TJ: You mean a character who's already been established?

PAM: That's an interesting distinction.

TJ: The vast majority of the time another character is introduced is because logically there would be another person there. Sometimes it's just a matter of thinking "Oh, it would be fun to have another roommate in this house since he/she might give us a couple more possible opportunities for interaction."

DAVID: And the rare times, when we might want to get rid of some of these people, would be if they were antagonistic because those characters are not helping us discover the scene we're in. We don't shy away from difficult moments, but it's happened that, at the very beginning of the show, I'm playing someone who is nothing but disagreeable. So that character left and someone else came in, so we could try it with these new guys.

TJ: More often than not, we would go to a character who's already been established because it's logical. For instance, if we think the waiter would be speaking right now, let's see the waiter. Otherwise, it's because we are trying to physically show the people who have the most interesting interaction going on between them.

If there is a table of four people at a restaurant, we don't need to hear Guy #4 order his tomato soup, tuna melt, and diet cola if we can hear Guy #1 say to Guy #2, "I don't have any money, man. I'm gonna need you to buy me dinner." We try to see what is more important.

DAVID: And we're not doing farce, so we don't try to keep everybody. We don't like the gimmick of jumping around and keeping everyone alive just for the sake of it.

PAM: Is there a change or evolution in pace that impresses upon how often you switch between characters?

DAVID: No plan or anything. Not consciously. We may end up falling into certain patterns, but we're not doing it intentionally ... because we're just doing the next little thing.

PAM: Even though you don't know when the end is going to be and you're not pre-planning, do you have conscious thoughts about which character you want to end with?

DAVID: We like to have it be at least one of the original folks. Probably 95% of our shows have at least one of them at the very end, because that's the story we first discovered. If we were to move from character to character, say, a guy goes to school and runs into a classmate, and that classmate goes to work and has a boss, and then we go home with the boss for dinner, we'll end up so far away from that original moment that there doesn't seem to be a need for those first several scenes. We're no longer discovering the scene we first stepped into.

PAM: Let's talk about holding onto your emotional point of view, like when a character, who is afraid of life, stays that way. What's the balance between holding onto your point of view and being open to change?

DAVID: There is no reason to "hold onto" an emotional point of view.

PAM: To maintain who you are as a character?

DAVID: Yes, but always be open to change.

PAM: So let's say your character is a jerk. He doesn't just start being nice out of the blue. But he might become nicer over the course of the show due to events that have occurred?

DAVID: Or in other situations, we find out he's a very caring guy. Just not in that situation.

TJ: Yeah. Scrooge can't throw the crown out the window on page three, y'know. It takes four ghosts and a thing. No one is going to think less of you if the impetus for your emotional change is strong enough to justify that change. It's when you change for no good reason that it's baloney. You establish who you are, but if there is reason to change, then there is reason to change.

DAVID: We don't like to think, "Oh, this guy needs to change, so we do it, even though he's got no reason." We'd rather the guy stay a jerk the entire time than be disingenuous.

16

INHABITING AND MAINTAINING SPACE

The most precious gift we can offer anyone is our attention.
— *Thich Nhat Hanh*

At the beginning of a *TJ & Dave* show, the stage is empty, save for a few chairs. By the end, the stage could be crowded with conjured spaces: a young couple's apartment, an office cubicle maze, a roadside, a bus station. As the lights come back up, the spaces slowly evaporate into the ethers of the audience's imaginations. An audience will watch TJ and David create an invisible yet real world onstage, piece by piece. David may reach out into the air to set a teacup onto an imaginary surface. Then TJ straightens some place settings on the same surface, and a dining table materializes. They accept and add to each other's creation of an onstage environment.

They say that there is nothing magical about their approach to space and object work. Rather, they simply attempt to pay very close attention to details while establishing a real world one step at a time.

TJ AND DAVID ON INHABITING SPACE

When we utilize and interact with space onstage, we're merely interacting as realistically as possible in the world in which we've found ourselves. That's so much easier than inventing some staged space or performing within a conceit of theatrical staging. The needs of the scene dictate the dimensions as opposed to catering to the needs of the audience. That's why if we're playing four people sitting around the dinner table, it's fairly logical that one guy would be sitting with his back to the audience. It's easier for us to agree to that reality than it is to figure if we'd need, say, two on one side diagonally and evenly spaced and two on the other side. Who has time or brain space for that? We sure don't.

Even if we did, that wouldn't look anything like a real family of four sitting down to a ham dinner. It may be nice if the audience could see everything, but at least they're able to *hear* everything. And maybe the scene is not about that guy with his back to the audience. Perhaps the audience could think of it as an over-the-shoulder shot in a movie.

Necessity, convenience, reality and ease are our guides, even if it means turning our backs to the audience. In a scripted play, typically a guy ordering a drink at a bar would be staged with the actors cheating out or surreptitiously side-by-side so the audience can see both actors' faces. We don't take on this theatrical presentation because it would be harder for us to read one another as precisely. Since we couldn't always see each other, we'd be denying ourselves information, and trying to pick up everything out of our periphery. Instead, we inhabit space as it would be in real life. It's just more natural to play it that way. We try to do what makes the most sense, and, if our backs are to the house, we try to be a little bit louder. We don't ever purposefully want people not to be able to hear, but that's how the bartender stands. He stands facing his patron. So that's how we stand.

As the geography of the world we're inhabiting is revealed, it becomes set, in much the same way the characters and their relationships become established facts. And as those facts are set, we'd better be paying attention to details—where did the other guy set down his mug? Where is the kitchen cupboard? We may very well be called upon to play that guy making a second cup of instant coffee in his efficiency dinette. And we are well aware that the audience has a far better perspective of the space we're living in than we do. They may not know exactly where the mug was, but they'll quickly notice that something is amiss if we pick it up from a different place. They'll notice if we walk through an ottoman or put our hand through the cupboard. We try never to do that.

We don't want to provide any reason for the audience to doubt what is going on. When we goof up, it takes us and the audience out of the show for a moment, so we find it behooves us to take note of our environment. Likewise, staged, theatrical elements would give an excuse to see the show as unreal. If we consider it all real, the audience will follow our lead. So the characters are considered to be real, the space is considered to be real, and the objects are considered to be real.

If we consider it all real, the audience will follow our lead.

Our goal to react reasonably and logically, moment by moment, applies to revealing our environment too. Even as we notice everything about the space discovered onstage, we still try not to overplay environment. Rarely would we dust a table to indicate its shape in real life. We won't touch something all the way around to establish it. If there is a table, we'll put a drink down on it. That is enough to indicate a table. We are not mimes trapped in a box. We merely are two guys knocking around the kitchen or doing Sudoku at a bus depot or having a smoke on the front porch of the house where we grew up.

There's also no point in under-indicating our object work or environment because we would not want to leave an undefined counter for our stage partner to walk into. TJ notes, "Sometimes David puts a coffee cup down on a table, and I don't know how big that table is yet. I won't know how big it is until maybe he gets up from the chair and walks around the thing. Then maybe I'll know it's an oval table. If he doesn't get up, I won't know all of its dimensions, but I can say I know its height. It's just a matter of paying attention, little by little as our environment makes itself known."

At first, this approach took effort and concentration. At some point, we realized that what's most genuine is when we do it without effort and concentration. When you put down this book and get up to grab a snack from the kitchen (wouldn't a piece of peach pie be nice right about now?), you're not going to concentrate deliberately on placing the book on a table, maneuvering around the furniture, carefully slicing a nice wedge of peach pie. You're just going to do it. We've discovered we can't do object work both honestly *and* too deliberately. So we've had to figure out a way to do it casually if we want anyone to believe it.

To that end, we find it useful to take our time. Sometimes improvisers rush through the job, and they end up doing object work in a shorthand way to indicate a fridge exists. We've all done it: swung open a refrigerator door so quickly that everything on the door shelves would fall, then, without glancing inside the fridge, grabbed a nondescriptly shaped something, and set it down on the counter-ish space. Then we'd have gone on to say whatever we were saying before we remembered we should probably make this stuff actual. To do it poorly is counterproductive; nobody believes it is real. Even though we don't consider ourselves especially gifted at or have any propensity for this type of pantomime, if we take a half-second to look at the sandwich we're about to pick up, it's *there*. If we take that moment to see it, then we might get the opportunity to discover it's not cut in half. Or we may see it is cut in half, and it's got a great, crispy edge on it, so we can handle it a little more heartily than if it wasn't toasted. In our experience, if you just take a second to see the objects before you, then you'll handle them specifically. Sometimes people go past that little moment because they're more worried about indicating "This is a sandwich" or "This is a refrigerator," as opposed to just having this be a refrigerator. Have this be a sandwich. Have this be a glass of soda and let the bubbles tickle your nose.

IN CONVERSATION: *SPACE AND "COFFEE THUMB"*

In this talk, we break down specific examples from past shows to evaluate how TJ and David approach environment and object work onstage.

PAM: You have made moves establishing space in your shows that nearly brought tears to my eyes.

DAVID: You're talking about TJ now, right?

PAM: No, both of you. And, actually, the moment I'm referring to is a move you made, David.

TJ: This is something that David did? I'm tuning out for a bit. Let me know when this part is over, and I'll get back to you.

PAM: Well, technically, you did this moment together...

TJ: Okay, I'm back.

DAVID: No, not yet.

PAM: At this show, you played a nephew and an uncle at a museum viewing an anatomy exhibit of the insides of a human. You were having an interaction with the guard, played at that moment by David too, at the door of the gallery before you went in. It was so graphic that TJ, who was playing the uncle at this point, started to feel like throwing up. He crossed the stage and switched back to cross again as if he was running around the exhibit cases out of the gallery towards the bathroom. And in the blink of an eye, David went from being the nephew at the exhibit to being the security guard posted outside the gallery, who TJ passes on his way out toward the bathroom. There was very little interaction between you two at that moment beyond maybe a nod or a little wave. There was no real reason David had to be standing there, playing the guard, but he did it.

DAVID: You don't have to make stuff up. What is reasonable given the set of circumstances? It's reasonable that guard is still standing there.

TJ: Pam, you say there is no reason David had to be standing there, but there is every and only one reason he should have been standing there: Because the guard would have been standing there.

PAM: According to the reality you established, he stands there. I was taught to think the only reason he stands there is for a potential interaction between the characters.

DAVID: The fact that there was no interaction gives tons of information.

PAM: That's true. The fact that the security guard didn't try to help says a lot about his personality or at least his approach to his work. Maybe running to the bathroom to barf is not so terribly unusual at this exhibit.

DAVID: Not doing anything is often exactly the right thing to do. Otherwise, the guard stops the Uncle and prevents him from going to vomit. And now we have an uninteresting *I Love Lucy* scene about him wanting to throw up and me not letting him.

TJ: Remember that other show, Dave? I think it was a show with John Lutz, and we were in a supermarket? I think someone was running to get from the top of aisle five to aisle four ...

DAVID: Yes. There were three crosses in a row, right?

TJ: Yeah. And we had kind of even forgotten about this one guy, who might have been a stocker or something like that. But as someone was running down that aisle, they looked back at the stocker. And it was a real quick interaction:

"Hey, John."
"Hey, Ray."

There was an enormous reaction from the audience. Even if those lines hadn't been spoken to each other, there still would have been an enormous reaction because that's where that guy was. And that's it. There wasn't anything funny said or done. It was just that's where that guy would have been.

There are a couple of reasons why those moments get a reaction. Part of it was audience delight, "This is real! The guy who was there twenty minutes ago is still there." There might be a little appreciation of our remembering those details, and there is a little reward to the audience for paying as close attention as we do. "I knew that stock boy was there, and, dammit, he's still there!" It's because they're watching, paying attention, and investing in it.

PAM: I don't remember how the rest of the audience reacted to that museum guard switch, but I was so delighted. That moment was the whole show for me. If you had stopped there, I would have been *completely* satisfied.

DAVID: Me too. Many times, the show, for me, is one tiny moment that nobody else is aware of. Maybe TJ, but that's about it.

PAM: And that's okay with you?

DAVID: Okay? Oh, it's great.

PAM: Have there been exercises or experiences as improvisers and actors that have helped you become better at object work?

DAVID: Certainly. Pay attention to what you really do when you drink out of a cup. Somebody said to me the other day, "It's so strange to see you drink coffee out of an actual cup." Apparently, they know me more from the shows than real life. So I said, "How am I doing?"

TJ: ... as real coffee dribbled all down your face when you put your thumb in your mouth.

DAVID: That never happens on Wednesday nights.

TJ (*sarcastically*)**:** Real coffee, I drink with my thumb knuckle in my lower lip.

DAVID: Again, it's just paying attention offstage, so that I don't have to pay attention onstage. This is just how I drink a cup of coffee. My hand is actually three inches from my face, not with my thumb on my chin.

PAM: Inspired by your object work, I've taken to noticing lately just how I put on a shirt. It turns out it doesn't just magically float above my head and fall effortlessly over my body when I raise up my arms. I always thought that's how a shirt is put on onstage. There are a lot of little movements that go into putting on a shirt.

TJ: Yes, and simultaneously, a lot is less intentional than it appears when you do it onstage. You don't necessarily look at every button as you put on a shirt. Or look at every button as you take off a shirt.

DAVID: And they don't magically always work right. There was this stand-up who used to do mime with real objects. So he'd have an actual banana in his hand, but he would peel it as if he were a mime doing it to a mimed banana. And it was just grotesque. He'd be using his whole body every time he peeled a section. So that is the other extreme, an over-indication of everything. That's not how we do it either. We attempt to do it as an actual person would do it.

TJ: And, if we're really good, as *the person we're playing* would do it.

PAM: Along that line, TJ amazed me during a show where he played an older man getting dressed. It was this little thing as he put on his pants; he wiggled his foot a little bit to ease the pant leg over it.

DAVID: Give me a call when you're done talking to TJ.

PAM: If I wanted to demonstrate to a student how to do object work, I would just show that scene. It seemed like you've studied how you put your on pants, and then applied it to that older man.

TJ: Maybe. My guess is that I thought that someone young and more flexible would lean over and just pull that pant leg up. If you don't have trouble bending, you'd just bend over and yank that thing. But if you're of an age when backs are sore and joints are tighter, you find a different way. In my imagination, you'd pull the pant leg from the top of the thigh with one hand and wiggle your foot through it. You wouldn't just reach down around mid-calf level and yank the rest of that fabric over your heel.

PAM: How much conscious thought goes into putting on clothes, or whatever object work you're doing?

TJ: There is some conscious aspect to it because that body is not my body (although it's quickly becoming my body). That character's body is a 74-year-old body, so there is some conscious thought to portraying it. But every once in a while, if you're really in it, it becomes your body. I'd like to be able to say that I didn't have a choice how I put on those pants because I *was* that man.

There is more conscious stuff when I play a woman because that's not who I am and not how my body normally moves. If I can get good enough and really disappear in someone, every once in a while I find something happening that doesn't feel conscious. It just feels like how they're doing it.

PAM: David, when I wanted to talk about space, you were a little surprised and said you and TJ have never discussed your treatment of space and object work. You've never rehearsed it. Is that right?

DAVID: Correct. I don't think we've had any discussion about it. We just do it. We do what we can to the best of our ability. It seems to be enough.

We have to find a way to do it realistically and therefore effortlessly if we want anyone to believe it. It's similar to indicating a brother-sister relationship by saying, "Oh, Sister," rather than treating her like someone you've known more intimately than anyone else for as long as you've been alive. The audience will figure out you're brother and sister. Those are the two choices: Do it. Or play at it.

TJ: Yeah, "play at it." That's exactly the phrase I was thinking.

PAM: All of this comes down to a hyper-awareness of the moment you are in.

TJ: Yeah, and I don't even know if you need "hyper." Don't play act eating a sandwich. Eat a goddamn sandwich. And truly, not to get nitpicky, but I don't know if it's "hyper," it's just not "*hypo* ..."

DAVID: Hypo? You mean the semi-aquatic mammal in Africa?

TJ: Yes, David. Yes, that's exactly what I mean.

17

DETAILS AND SPECIFICITY

I always wanted to be somebody,
but now I realize I should have been more specific.

—Lily Tomlin

Work with an improvisation teacher and chances are you'll soon hear their views on the importance of providing specificity and details in the work. It is widely believed that more specificity makes better improvisation. "How 'bout one for the road, barkeep?" is more helpful than "I'd like something to drink." Details and specifics color a scene and provide loads of information about characters and relationships, which can often make the audience laugh.

In *TJ & Dave* you see charming and unique instances of specificity in scene work that seem to arise naturally. Who is this person willing to go toe-to-toe with his boss over the office softball game, willing to risk his job over a casual sporting event? How will his colleagues react to his drawing a line in the sand? The whole show reveals the answers. And it has nothing to do with merely providing specifics, and everything to do with representing real life, specifically.

TJ AND DAVID ON DETAILS

For us, specificity comes from noticing rather than inventing. Details arise as needed as we act and speak naturally and honestly. In real life, people are naturally specific. We try to portray them as such onstage. Implementing specificity doesn't require special training as much as awareness of what we, as social creatures, are doing all the time. Rather than willfully tacking details onto a scene, we believe that it is the improviser's job to listen for the specifics being revealed over the course of the scene. Then we allow them to educate us about who we already are to each other.

Specifics are useful because they provide information. If TJ's character says, "Hand me that 5/16th," we both have learned a tremendous amount about that person. For one thing, he has twelve different wrenches; otherwise, he would have just said, "Hand me that wrench." And the other character's reaction—whether it's to grab the correct wrench without hesitation or a stony silence with arms akimbo or a panicked rummaging through the toolbox—informs us terrifically too. It's important to let the reality of the scene determine our use of specifics. We would not say, "Hand me that 5/16th" just for fun or to show off our comfortable relationship with hand tools. Those details arise for a reason: to provide information about the scene, the character, and the relationship between the characters. The specifics in and of themselves are not essential in a scene.

We approach specifics as a way of informing us about the dynamics of the relationship and our emotional points of view. (In other words, the Heat and the Weight.) If we're trying to learn about the nature of the relationship in a scene and we hear a wife character say in a formal way to her husband, "Oh, hello *Jeffrey*. What a lovely red shirt you are wearing," then our internal antennae would twitch. Typically, a wife doesn't use her husband's given name and that level of specificity in casual conversation. Using his name and mentioning the shirt and its color would need to mean something. There is something up in this relationship at this moment, and we'll be listening very carefully to see what the scene reveals it to be. Maybe it is Valentine's Day and Jeffrey forgot, *again*? Maybe they had a huge financial windfall and are practicing a newfound, forced formality? Maybe he's going on a covert rendezvous with that green-haired barista he flirts with?

> **Let the reality of the scene determine our use of specifics.**

On the other side of that coin, when we don't find ourselves using specifics at the top of a scene, we are informed by that as well. If only "Oh, hello" is spoken, perhaps we're total strangers, or we're completely intimate and nothing else needs saying. (Here is an opportunity to employ Ockham's razor. Our instincts will be to consider the obvious first.) The way it is said will lead us to form a better idea of what it means.

Our first responsibility is to notice the details as they're being uncovered. We aren't declaring them. We aren't creating them. We're just noticing them as they appear and then living in that ever-forming reality. Just about everybody does something for a reason, including providing details. For example, a woman stands up and crosses the room to water the basil plant. Why did she pick that moment to water the basil? More than likely, there was something particular going on in her mind that made her do this certain action. It could have been anything from "This is what I do at two o'clock" to "What that person said made me feel like I'm dying, so I'm going to make sure that something in this world is alive." All these details are clues to help us discover the scene we're playing. Like every other aspect of our approach to improvisation, as the details are discovered, they become true. If we inhabit a world that is real and detailed for us, then hopefully it will be real and detailed for everyone.

> **Just about everybody does something for a reason, including providing details.**

We must act as participants as well as observers in the scene. As with object work, it's as simple as taking the briefest of moments to notice the world around us. We're paying attention to what our scene partner is doing and to what we're doing, how we're doing it, and why we're doing it. Sometimes improvisers will make a stage-cross because they think the scene feels too static; or they're anxious in the spot they're holding, so they make a non-specific cross to the other side of the stage. And that's how it will be perceived ... as non-specific. If we take the time to realize whether we're crossing that stage to go feed the fish or to grab the rest of the coffee in our cup, we find it better informs us. We're going to move differently for each scenario. Feeding the guppies may be a chore that needs to be done (and should have been done by the kids, dammit), while getting those last sips in the "World's Best Dad" mug might be an act of desperation to stay awake until the kids get home (and it's already forty-five minutes past their curfew, dammit). Knowing precisely why we're doing something adds an informed aspect to our movements, our language, and our relationship dynamic. Even if the audience or our stage partners don't know why we're crossing the stage, it will still read as informed because we know why we're doing it. Someone playing with this level of mindful intention is way more intriguing to watch, and play with, than someone who is making unfounded decisions or actions ... regardless of how specific they are.

As the details are discovered they become true.

This idea of moving with purpose applies to providing details too. Suppose TJ's character wants to get across to David's character that every time he speaks, it feels like it's killing a little part of him. TJ might end up saying just something simple like, "Yeah." But he's going to say it precisely in a way that tries to get that other thing across. It is our opinion that to think specifically causes you to act specifically ... and to act specifically causes that specific reality to be better revealed. (Read that one a couple times ... we know, it's a mouthful.) So we try to take a half-second to notice why we're saying "Yeah."

We try hard not to let words get in the way of communication. In the basil example, if someone says, "I'm going to go water the plants," what might she really be saying? "I don't want to be here anymore"? "I want something to be alive"? "I think we should cook at home more"? Maybe she means "I won't let you kill off the Italian parts of me that still remain." Specifics and details in improvisation are yet another reason acute listening can only benefit our work. Listen to the words and the meaning beneath the words. We're listening for specifics and the omission of specifics. We suggest you listen for what people are actually saying when they talk.

To think specifically causes you to act specifically.

As much as we find details in a scene informative, we see dangers in providing too many. For us, providing specificity just for the hell of it poses a problem that we dearly want to avoid: being an unhelpful scene partner. It is difficult to play with someone who is merely providing a laundry list of specifics that don't inform the scene. We'd be jumping to unintended conclusions. We'd be on different pages. In different scenes.

Excessive or mindless use of specificity interferes with our partner's realizations as to who they are. Preserving our partner's autonomy is essential, so we try to be careful of both the way we speak and the way we read the meaning behind what our partner says. The more we impose specifics on our scene partners, the less freedom we allow them. It's the difference between saying, "That's a huge rhino head on the wall," and "You are a big game hunter." We don't want to use specifics to drive the scene, determine who our scene partner is, or to make them react according to our agenda. There is a balance between providing reasonable specificity and being controlling, and we are careful to walk that fine line with respect and attention.

> **Preserving our partner's autonomy is essential.**

Let's say we're in a scene when TJ says, "Don and his pipe, huh?" This statement is plenty specific and leaves his partner free to interpret as he wishes. On the other hand, "What do you think of Don's newfound professor getup since he got that teaching gig?" feels too pushy and constrictive. Some of it is needless exposition; and regardless, it's not how people talk in real life. Two people who know each other well would only need to say, "Don and his pipe, huh?" and they'd know what they're talking about. If we're paying attention, we'll know who Don is to us by the delivery of the words. "Don and his pipe, huh?" is still specific without being overt for the sake of exposition or making sure we're all on the same page or writing a script for our scene partner. "Don and his pipe, huh?" gives us all those great, implied details about our buddy Don—his weird professorial getup and that obnoxious pipe—but in a more elegant and realistic fashion.

We show respect for each other's autonomy onstage. TJ illustrates the point using the above scene:

If I say, "Don and his pipe, huh?" in a certain way, Dave knows that I'm excited about it, which doesn't necessarily mean he has to be. I'm just letting him know that I'm jazzed about it. But whatever has excited me about this change in Don doesn't need to be exciting to Dave. He may hate that Don's become flamboyant and full of himself. While I see it as much-needed self-confidence, he sees it as Don being real uppity now.

By allowing our partner the freedom to interpret, we open the scene to myriad lovely opportunities, rather than forcing one person's preconceived idea onto another. As you know, our goal is to discover, not invent, the scene we are in. The easiest way to respect our stage partner is to think and speak as specifically as we do in real life, while allowing them the autonomy to react however they may.

IN CONVERSATION: *GIFT GIVING*

Joy in looking and comprehending is nature's most beautiful gift.
— *Albert Einstein*

That's the biggest gift I can give anybody:
Wake up, be aware of who you are, what you're doing
and what you can do to prevent yourself from becoming ill.
— *Maya Angelou*

Improvisers are often instructed to give gifts to each other, such as the gift of providing details that inform a scene, move it forward, or otherwise help out. While some see an opening line such as "Ah, Princess Cavanaugh, you're looking resplendent in your jousting tournament finery" as a welcome gift to begin a scene full of detail and specificity, TJ and David most certainly do not. They have a different view of what constitutes a gift in improvisation.

TJ: Anything that gives me more information and understanding is a gift. But the idea behind improvisational gift-giving usually refers to some sort of endowment, like, "All right, General!" which I tend to think is always a gift you'd want to return.

PAM: Because the other player endowed you with being a general as a sort of tacked on invention?

TJ: Yeah. Rather than being endowed with something, I like being able to choose for myself. I can offer something to David and how he reacts to it is his gift to me. That's an autonomous thing. I don't want to take away any of David's freedom by determining for him who he is. I don't want to label it.

PAM: So reaction is a gift?

TJ: Yes. But I think any piece of information, including silence to a line, is a kind of gift.

PAM: It sounds like what you're saying is that you don't think improvisers should focus on giving gifts but rather on receiving them?

TJ: Sure, but you don't have to be intentional with the gift. Doing something is going to be a gift. I guess we're talking about unlearning the popular usage of the term. If the gift is "Man, that's a fancy, new tweed jacket you're wearing," that's a lay-on.

PAM: It takes away your autonomy as an improviser.

TJ: Right. As opposed to just "Good morning, Ray." That's a gift enough to me. David's intentional and focused participation in a scene is the only gift I could ask for or need. I don't need him to describe my age, build, appearance ....

DAVID: To behave consistently and reasonably is the gift. I honestly don't know what "giving a gift" means. TJ and I don't talk about gifts. The goal is to behave reasonably in the situation, and then we'll determine better what the situation is. I don't know that there are gifts, really. If someone comes up to me and says I'm their cousin with one arm—that's not a gift. That doesn't have anything to do with *anything*. I often find that when people are talking about giving a gift, they've got their heads up their asses.

> **To behave consistently and reasonably is the gift.**

TJ: It's like, "Sister Teresa, everyone here at the convent has heard about your abortion."

DAVID: Yeah. That's not a gift. That's a sentence I have to serve.

TJ: That speaks again to the importance of preserving our partner's autonomy.

PAM: Sometimes onstage, my partner will say something that clarifies for me.

DAVID: I don't see that as a gift. There is no giving. No giver. There is only the realization that something was revealed, and *that* is wonderful.

PAM: As I understood it, the gift is when you see new information, acknowledge it, and use it.

> **The only gift you could ask for is someone's active and fully immersed participation in a scene.**

TJ: It doesn't have to be boxed and wrapped in a bow for it to be a gift. A waitress puts down two pieces of pie in front of us, and Dave doesn't wait for me to start digging into the thing. That's a gift to me. That's a piece of information that sheds a little more light on who we are to each other. It's not, "Man, it's good to take a break. We've been working on this house,

Ray. You're a great foreman." That's what we usually hear referred to when someone says, "Oh, what a great gift he gave me." But I don't consider that a gift. That guy just boxed me.

The only gift you could ask for is someone's active and fully immersed participation in a scene. Knowing he's paying attention; that's the only gift you can ask of a partner.

PAM: In the earlier story of the "Chill Phil" show, TJ delivered the first line in a very specific, emotional way. With admiration and a little frustration, he said, "Friggin' Chill Phil." To me, that's an example of a huge and wonderful gift: clarity.

DAVID: I guess it's just terminology. Personally, I don't find those terms helpful. Part of it is the basic notion of how we look at the show. If we truly believe this scene is revealing itself to us, we're not in a position to give anything. We're only in a position to notice.

> **We're not in a position to give anything.**
> **We're only in a position to notice.**

TJ: Internal to a show, we don't think about gifts. We might call it information or a reaction. You can almost substitute "partnership in this discovery" or "another piece of information" or "a slightly better understanding of who we are" for "gift." To my ears, that word has become instilled with other meanings and treatment in how improvisers use it.

PAM: So you don't find the common usage of the idea of giving gifts to be useful to you?

TJ: As Dave and I look at it, our only gift exchange comes before the show. It's the tacit agreement that we have a dedicated and invested partner to explore this thing we're about to embark on. That's the gift we give each other. During the show, everything else that happens is just the living up to that little gift of "I'm here with you."

18

IMPROVISATION AT THE SPEED OF LIFE

> Nature does not hurry.
> Yet everything is accomplished.
>
> *– Lao Tsu*

TJ and David weren't sure there was much to say about the pacing of their show. Yet, when people describe *TJ & Dave,* one of the first things mentioned is the unhurried pace. They talk about how TJ and David seem to take their time. There are weighty pauses and rich silences in their show. Time and space are allowed for reactions and reflection. But neither views their show as necessarily slow.

Some call the duo's style "slow comedy," a term bandied about to represent a form of improvisation that tends to be more patient, more relationship-based, and less plot-based, less wacky. You can find other slow comedy shows out there, but if you wander into a typical improvisation theater on a typical night, you'll likely find fast and furious shows that leave you in awe of the improvisers. Some are naturally quick-witted, others feel the need to be fast, and still others speed up from the joy and adrenaline from performing before an audience. That's awe-inspiring, fun and entertaining as hell ... but TJ and David take a very different approach.

TJ AND DAVID ON PACING

In most every chapter of this book, we've talked about making our show like life, natural and credible and true. Our approach to character development is simply the result of attempting to portray believable people. Our approach to object work stems from our efforts to have those people live in real (albeit imagined) worlds onstage. In fact, we approach all of improvisation as an effort to discover—and uncover—actual moments already occurring. Maybe that's why this chapter is towards the end of the book, even though it's one of the first things people tend to remark on when they talk about our show. To us, pacing is just another example in our effort to represent real life onstage.

Life moves at a variety of speeds. Sometimes it's fast. Sometimes it's slow. And the fact that you recognize that it's fast or slow seems to suggest that there is a regular pace of life most of the time. Spend a day with someone. See if she's frantic all the time or unrelentingly glacial. (If she is, then see if you can spend a second day with her.) We don't know about you, but the vast majority of our days are carried out at a fairly moderate pace. In *TJ & Dave*, we are likely not going to have to deal with a comet hitting the earth. We are much more likely to end up in a regular day in someone's regular life with issues and concerns that are specific to them. And some regular things, almost by definition, tend to be set at a deliberate pace.

People often refer to *TJ & Dave* as slow comedy. And though it might end up being both "slow" and "comedy," we don't think either word applies particularly aptly to our show. We don't step onstage to be either deliberately slow or comedic. Ideally, the show moves how life is supposed to move. Rather than thinking about ticks of the clock, we try to play the scene with integrity. We try not to step on an honest moment in favor of something invented. We focus on discovering a grounded reality rather than sticking to a formula for pursuing what's funny. Regardless of pace, we think *all* improvisation, at its best, can have integrity and believability, and the pursuit of honesty. Whatever term folks want to stick on it, approaching improvisation one little step at a time is the way we like to improvise. And to be perfectly candid, it's the way we improvise best. Neither one of us considers himself to be especially quick or one-liner funny. But we're certainly not trying to set out to do a show in first gear ... unless we happen to find ourselves in a show that calls for first gear. But that would be a reaction to what the show is calling for rather than a preordained intent.

> **The show moves how life is supposed to move.**

We wonder if the pace of our show is actually more a matter of perception. We are big admirers of the lovely choice to respond with silence. And that might seem, on the surface, as going slowly. But it's not. It has nothing to do with pace. There's not a lot of talking, but *plenty* is still going on. We can just play reality, which often isn't frantic or frightened or wordy. Maybe that comes off as slow.

For example, in a recent show, there was a moment when a dying lady looked at her offspring, who were carrying on a conversation. The lady wasn't saying anything. For us, that was one of the highlights of the show: just a lady looking at the people who came to visit her and enjoying their company. No words. No movement. But *tons* of stuff going on. We didn't experience that part of the show as slow in the least.

We enjoy giving breath to moments of reaction. In most television shows the frame is centered on the person speaking, while, in films, viewers are often allowed to focus on the person(s) listening. We think of our show in more cinematic terms. We find it more interesting to watch how the listener is being affected. Perhaps this perceived slow pace is also a matter of allowing ourselves to be affected ... which often takes a silent beat or two.

Sometimes the information coming to you in a show (and in life) doesn't need to be pondered or wondered about, so we keep in mind that not everything is owed a weighty beat. The routines and rhythms of certain activities click along at a pretty quick pace. Sure, if you're in a heavy conversation, it will move more slowly because those ideas deserve a little *gravitas*. But if someone says, "Do you want milk in your coffee?" we know the answer pretty quickly. If the music is on way too loudly, we turn it down right away. If a person we love is in trouble, we don't hesitate to try and help. Things don't necessarily have to move slowly for the sake of saying that we're playing with intent or playing honestly. Sometimes our truth is readily at hand, and sometimes it takes a beat.

Although we usually don't intentionally manipulate the pace one way or another in *TJ & Dave*, we have noticed some patterns that tend to occur over the course of a typical show. The top of a show is one place we definitely don't find ourselves rushing unnecessarily. In some cases, the Heat and Weight are immediately clear, so we won't wait to act on it. Those shows might shoot right out of the starting gate. But in other cases, the show is still revealing itself, so we try to provide some time and space. Some shows might even take twenty minutes to make themselves known. Because in those first moments of a show, our education is starting brand new, and at that point we're just learning our numbers and our shapes, so to speak. Once we're further into a show, we're further along in our education. We tend to know a lot more about ourselves and each other, so we may be more likely to move a bit more quickly. At the beginning of a show, you could ask us if two and two are four, but we're not sure. We'll need to take a moment to think about it; we don't yet know what two and two even are in this world, so we'll need to take a moment to think about it. Later on, when we do know, we can answer that question immediately.

Recently, we did a show where the beginning formed pretty quickly. It was a real simple feel. And immediately we knew, "Oh, we're co-workers. We're of this particular age. We're two guys. We're standing in a store." There weren't even any words yet. It wasn't magic; we were just paying attention to the show that quickly revealed itself. Both of our hands were conveying something. Both of our stances were meaning something. Our proximity was saying something, the way we were moving a little bit, the looks on our faces ... immediately, we got all the information we needed to know about who we were to each other in order to start the scene. We assumed we were correct, and in doing so we immediately were correct.

Now we're about to contradict ourselves a wee bit, just to keep you on your toes (and because life's a bitch like that). There does tend to be one matter in pacing that is fairly conscious for us. In *TJ & Dave*, we tend to have the whole show play out in actual time. That is, the clock is running equally in all the scenes, and one minute in life equals one minute in every character's life in the show. Let's say we go from a scene between two female friends draining a box of wine while commiserating about a romance gone sour to a scene where a few office workers are playing a game of "Two Truths and a Lie." When we leave the office workers and return to those women, time has gone by. We pick up again with those ladies after however many minutes we were in the office, during which time they've probably made a dent in that tasty box of pink Zinfandel.

There are rare exceptions when we manipulate time, such as a flash-forward or flashback, but it's pretty uncommon in *TJ & Dave*. We do a time dash of even a few minutes maybe once every fifteen shows, if that. But if we find the show calls for a time dash, we won't stop ourselves from doing it. Perhaps it's a matter of expediency. For example, we'll skip over the few minutes it takes someone to exit the bar, get across the street, go into the office building, take the elevator, and find the boss's office. We'll go straight from him exiting the bar to walking through the boss's door. (Out of sheer practical matters, walking is one of the oddest things for us to portray. On a stage, a dude crossing the street by himself is going to look funky no matter how you slice it.) Maybe if we had the luxury of a three- or four-hour show and a stage the size of a city block, and tons of supernumeraries, we wouldn't find it necessary to ever veer from real time.

We find this phrase "speed of life" kind of pithy, obviously for the sort of Einsteinian aspect to it. To be clear, "life," as opposed to "speed," is the more important part of that phrase. Quite frankly, one of our worries about trying to write something about longform in the first place is that basically, the way we see it, we're just trying to live life, but we're doing it onstage. So how do you write a book about living life and translate that to the stage? Improvisation is just life onstage (but more fun). Sometimes it's leisurely. Sometimes it's more harried. But, ideally, it's always real.

IN CONVERSATION: *We Think and Talk of Time*

Time is but the stream I go a-fishing in.
— *Henry David Thoreau*

Maybe it's not just the sweep of the second hand but rather the way an improviser thinks of time that alters the pace of a show? Let's zero in on the idea of different perceptions of time and how that affects the work.

PAM: How does the amount of time in *TJ & Dave* change your approach?

TJ: It's luxuriant.

DAVID: Oh, you mean time as in the length of the show? I thought you meant the time you put in, like a prison sentence.

PAM: How many more years do you have to serve?

DAVID: We're not sure. That's the terrible part of purgatory.

TJ: You know what's weird? The time served is torture. The time I'm serving today is lovely.

PAM: People talk a lot about the pace of your show.

DAVID: They should do something else. They should stop talking about the pace of our show and get out there and help the old lady across the street, goddammit. But that's what's wrong with these kids today.

PAM: How can an improviser approach a thirty-minute scene or even a three-minute scene with the same mindset that you use in your hour-long show?

DAVID: The same thing is true. If I'm improvising, I don't know what's going to happen. That's the truth. And that's *fine*.

PAM: But how about the "next little step" idea? I think some people might worry that in a three-minute scene they won't have time to get to the "good stuff" quickly enough.

DAVID: You mean when the chickens mutiny or some other *fascinating* thing like that?

PAM: Exactly.

DAVID: You're right. You won't get to that.

PAM: But if we're taking it slowly, we might not get to the heart of the scene in three minutes.

DAVID: Well, what else are you gonna do? What are the other options? To make up a bunch of nonsense? Or shoehorn stuff in there? Or have some preconceived notion that has nothing to do with the actual scene you're in? Those are the other options.

I think the way we look at it, there really aren't any other options. Because of the form, either I have other information or I don't have any information yet. But I only have the amount of information that I have. Even if I only know that we're brothers and we didn't get along and your name is Kippy, I'm going to behave that way. And since we're brothers that don't get along and your name is Kippy, I'm going to say it that way ... I'm going to say *[taking on a sneering tone]*, "*Kippy.*" That's about all I need to know. And the audience already knows all that. All they are going to see is two people behaving realistically given a certain set of circumstances. That's all I can do.

PAM: In forms of improvisation that don't fall under the "slow" category, players spend quite a bit of time worrying about speed. "Quickly get out your who, your what, and your where at the top of the show," "Come on with something immediately," "Initiate something the moment you walk onstage ...." It's all about getting it done quite quickly. They're thinking about pace a lot.

TJ: They're trying to get out what they *think* they need quickly—their facts—so they can begin playing. But you can start to play at the beginning and let those things show themselves.

DAVID: Right. It's antithetical to our way of playing. I think they jam all that stuff in the beginning so they can get all the facts out of the way, then they're comfortable. Then they can improvise because they know who they are, what they want, what they need, and where they are. Everybody needs those things ... but they already have them.

PAM: They *think* they need them.

DAVID: They think they don't have them. It's true that you can't improvise freely if you're afraid that you don't have those things. But either you don't have to find out all those things, or you already know it all.

19

THE THINGS WE CAN CONTROL

One of the many rewards of being a *TJ & Dave* fan is becoming aware of the rituals surrounding the show. There is a certain buzz in the air just before the show. You might catch TJ and David hugging before they take the stage. Longtime fans sing along as the opening Ike Reilly song ramps up—"Black Kat" in Chicago or the classic, "Commie Drives a Nova," when playing out of town. Halfway through that song, TJ and David take the stage, but savvy audience members hold their applause, knowing the song will play in its entirety. David paces off the area as they narrow their focus to only the world on the stage they are about to explore.

When TJ stands downstage with his hands shielding his eyes, methodically scanning the faces in the crowd, regulars know the show is about to start. Their theater is small enough that he can make eye contact with each and every audience member, eyebrows raising at recognition of some, sometimes a mouthed greeting or a smile and a nod. This ritual is a way to connect with the audience, a reminder that we're all about to take this journey into the unknown together.

DAVID AND TJ ON RITUALS

There are some things we try to do before and after every show that we feel tends to give us the best chance to have a decent program that night. Because we have so little power over the body of the show, we attempt to control a few things around it that bring us some sense of comfort or familiarity. These habits are certainly not unique to us, but for anyone who may find them of interest, they go a little something like this ...

We prefer to avoid having the first time we see a stage being when we are performing on it. If we are going up in an unfamiliar theater, we will give ourselves some time during the day to get acquainted with its space. We walk the stage end to end, back and forth, checking the lighting onstage for dim or hot areas as well as audience sight lines. One of us will go out to the deepest and widest parts of the house to check if we can be heard well enough. These are basic formalities, but it helps to know if a back row can't see us when we are seated onstage or if our faces will be dark when we play way downstage. We also try to get the room as cool as possible. Improvisation seems best served cold, and between stage lights and body heat, a room can get pretty warm over the course of an hour. All these elements are our way of knowing what there is to know about a space.

Regardless of whether we are in an unfamiliar place or not, we get to the green room a half hour before the show, get dressed, and then just hang out. We'll catch each other up on our day or week or anything that comes to mind. As it gets close to the show, we may do something slightly more physical: throw darts, dance. These days, we often play catch in a pitch-black room or dim park with one of those lighted balls designed for dogs. At about five minutes to curtain, the stage manager plays "The Ex-Americans" by Ike Reilly, and we go our separate ways. Once the song starts, we know we are heading into the show. It's our T minus five minutes and counting. We each have a private ritual, unknown even to each other, which we would prefer to keep that way. (And it would be bad manners for you to ask.) Suffice it to say, it's designed to calm and open our minds and bodies so that we can, hopefully, be sensitive antennae and expressive partners. The goal for all of this is to be more present during the show.

Just before we take the stage, we come back together and hug. We go up halfway through another Ike Reilly song and just hang around up there. We say a thing or two to each other about having a nice time tonight ... or we may not. The audience sometimes claps; sometimes they sit silently confused as to why we're up there while the music is still playing. This part of the process serves as an introduction to the dynamic of the show. They're learning that they're going to have to participate as more than just passive observers. We're all in this together, and we're going to find out what the show is at the same time. In a way, it's our invitation to the audience to come along for the ride. The primary reason we go up partway through the song, which will play to its conclusion, is to give us all a little chance to get acquainted with each other and this particular night. It's a bit like hopping in a pool. It may feel cold at first, but with a little time, we become accustomed to it. During these couple minutes, when Ike is singing but the show has not yet begun, we all hopefully get used to the water and move into the show a little more comfortably.

When the song ends, we do a short intro that always concludes with an honest appeal to "Trust us, this is all made up." Since we do not take a suggestion from the audience, we ask people to trust that we truly are improvising. We are showing respect for the audience's intellect and asking that they have some faith in us too.

"Trust us, this is all made up."
Lights go out. We let go.

The lights quickly come back up, launching us into the big chunk of the evening we can't control.

About fifty minutes later, the lights go out again, and then back up, and we are again in charge. We thank everybody, and we mean it. We are thankful for their participation and support throughout the evening. And we take off.

Trust us, this is all made up.

Back in the green room, we spend some more time together to transition between the spaces. When we're performing together for that hour, it feels like we've gone away for a while, like the bubble seals. For that time onstage, we are entirely immersed in each other and the revealed world. It's not an option to break the fourth wall because that wall is a wall, or that wall is a vista to a canyon ten miles away. We can't come back to this world too quickly, or we get the bends. Back in the green room, we go through the show with a special focus on the beginning, to see if we got it right, if we were true to the initial moments. Then we go through the rest of the show to check if we missed anything and figure why we screwed up where we did. Then we fight until someone is knocked to their knees. (Surprisingly, it works out to be about 50/50 who drops first.) After that, we stumble out into the night.

None of these little practices are all that stunning, but they help us relax, free ourselves, and be present. We find it helpful to have a bit of a routine. There is probably something to the normalcy of a certain regimen that quiets the mind and provides a sense of semi-safety. Ideally, a show should feel a little perilous. We're not trying to take away that lovely element of danger but to get ourselves to a place where we feel equipped to deal with the unknown ahead.

Outside of actual theatrical doings, during a typical week, we will sometimes rehearse, again with a special focus on our beginnings. We try to read, learn, look, listen, live a little.

And on show night, we try not to wear the same color shirt.

PART FIVE

OTHER SHOW STRUCTURES

20

PRACTICAL APPLICATIONS
(Not *TJ & Dave* Shows)

As this sentence is being written, another improvisational form is being created somewhere in the world. Most of you do not have the opportunity/burden/luxury of improvising with just one other person for about an hour, uninterrupted. You're more likely performing with a group doing a Harold or Montage or Deconstruction or theater games or the form you just invented and named. You may think these concepts we have been talking about are limited to the conditions of only our particular show. We feel that conclusion is erroneous. Further, you can implement these ideas in many other styles of shows.

Certainly, each show has different requirements: monologue deconstruction is beholden to the monologue; and a Harold to its opening. Still, a lot of the basics discussed so far apply to most every structure an improviser encounters. We always need to listen. We always need to pay attention. We always need to be as honest within the scenes as we possibly can. These are improvisation habits we can bring to any form, any show. Here's TJ and David on some things they find useful:

KNOW THE SHOW

No matter which show, it's important, first and foremost, to know what the form wants to do. Know your show. Players need to know both the concrete framework of the show and the intent of the show. Those are two separate things. The concrete framework is the structural outline. Often when people describe a form, they only describe that first part, the infrastructure and stylistic elements. They might describe their form like this: "We start with a character monologue; then that character does scenes with a second character; then character two does a monologue; then a scene with a third character, and so forth." That's only how the show moves. But what is the intent of the show? That second part is more important .... "What does the form seek to explore?" and "How can a show move most efficiently and artistically so that idea can be explored?"

For instance, we could describe the structure of *TJ & Dave* as "a fifty-minute one act that takes place in real time. Every character has either been mentioned or inferred. And the two players can establish and swap characters."

Those things are true. However, we would never describe it as that. To us, it is the investigation of a simple moment as the lights come up. For us, everything is dictated from that. We follow that wherever it seems to lead. The so-called structure is very different from the intent. And, in this case, unrelated.

THE HAROLD

There are many different long form improvisational structures, and the Harold is the granddaddy of them all. It is viewed as the classic form and the jumping off (or jumping away from) point for most other types of longform improvisation. The legendary Del Close and his fellow members of The Committee first explored the Harold in the late '60s in San Francisco. It wasn't until the mid-1980s, when he and Charna Halpern founded iO Theater (then ImprovOlympic), that Close developed and formalized this structure in earnest. He worked with students in workshops, like the ones David attended, which eventually led to the formation of the first official Harold teams, beginning with Baron's Barracudas.

The strict Harold in its current form starts with an opening, then has three scenes, a group game, a revisiting of the first three scenes, another group game, and then some sense of confluence:

Opening
Scenes A1, B1, and C1
Group Game
Scenes A2, B2, and C2
Group Game
Scenes A3, B3, and C3

That's how it moves. But what the Harold seeks to explore (its intent) is how to turn a single idea into a variety of themes and ideas through this group exploration.

In a Harold, improvisers unite to create a group mind, wherein the whole is greater than the sum of the parts. A Harold explores themes, notices patterns and allows them to weave together. But, first and foremost (and this often is forgotten), a Harold is good scene work.

The Harold's opening is far more than a warm up. It's here that the group starts to communicate as one while the suggestion is being dissected. It's not a matter of what eight or ten individuals are offering individually but what eight or ten individuals are creating as a cooperative unit. They are listening and responding to one another. It is not helpful to regard this opening as a place for jokes to be shoehorned in, which is tempting, but rather a place of honest impulse. Every idea discovered and explored during the opening is all the material we need for the rest of the Harold. We don't need any more content; in fact, it would not serve us. What we already have is more than enough. Whatever was uncovered and fleshed out in the opening are the blocks from which we must build the rest of the Harold. We're not getting any more deliveries of material, so we better make good use of that opening (i.e., listen).

Harold was not designed to tell stories. The scenes are not supposed to wrap up neatly, they "tend toward one another." Nor do we need to address the suggestion directly. We find that, through no effort on our part, ideas and people that seemed so unrelated at the beginning of a show begin to feel a resonance with each other through continued exploration of those things separately. We need to trust in the form, we need not exert our will on it. When everything goes well in a Harold, the connections occur almost like magic, like the show has a will of its own.

That's what a Harold requires of us. Likewise, other forms have their own structures and intents.

MONOLOGUE DECONSTRUCTION

This structure begins with a monologue, which leads into a series of scenes inspired by that monologue.

That's the concrete framework for the structure. But what does it seek to explore? Del expressed an interest in a dynamic that would contrast the autonomy of an individual mind with the gestalt intelligence of a group mind.

When delivering a monologue in one of these shows, the main responsibility is to be honest and to provide performers with some initial information. Any form should provide the opportunity for great scene work, and the function of monologues is to give enough information and meat for the cast to go out and do some very good scenes.

As the monologist, trying to entertain in any way, shape, or form is the least important task. If the story ends up being funny or interesting, it's a happy accident.

SHORTFORM

In short forms, the structure will likely place requirements upon the players. You may need to stop and sing your want, or rhyme all your dialogue, or continue your scene in an assigned emotion. The structure may also include plenty of audience participation. In form, these games were made to excite an audience by seeing their input incorporated immediately and offer instant results in a really funny way. But the intent of these games is to do a very good scene that just happened to have these other structural requirements.

You can do 26 lines of dialogue alphabetically in a row, but if they don't make sense or have some scenic connection between the characters, then there is no point. As we were taught, shortform games are to be played as scenes first. These are merely scenes with conditions. So do a good scene. Listen and respond honestly, consistent with the established reality.

This next little step idea is applicable in shortform scene work. Playing a game where we have to play the scene in different film, TV, or literary genres is a good example. If, say, we're directed to play the scene in a film noir style, we might think of how a 1940s detective would respond to the last initiation or line of dialogue. Or if given a sci-fi genre and you're playing a robot, you can still consider how a robot might respond to someone saying that they miss their family when a robot doesn't have one. It's just the same next little step idea but with a certain style.

TRANSFORMATIONAL FORMS

To take an example of another style in general and specific, let's talk transformational forms and a show done in Chicago called *J.T.S. Brown*, which was directed by Craig Cackowski. Structurally these transformational forms are often either described as seemingly formless or a collection of devices that lead to organic expression. And, again, that is only how it moves. What does the show want to explore by moving that way? *J.T.S. Brown* is a wide-open form that uses dream logic to flow from one reality to another. There are many devices associated with *J.T.S. Brown*—The Third Degree (a literal interrogation of a character); Telescoping (moving through a scene to another and another, then going back through those scenes to the original); or Morphing (entering and assuming another character, almost like pouring your body into theirs)—but what the form seeks to explore is much groovier than merely employing a variety of moves. Craig says the premise of the show is that "anything is possible in improv through group support. When players feel supported, they're encouraged to act on any impulse, without second guessing whether something is appropriate or allowed in a form."

The stylistic elements (how the show moves through dream logic) are there to support the ideas we want to explore, which is what can happen when a player feels fully supported.

We must know the show in order to understand our job in it.

To know our show, we need to focus on both the concrete and the conceptual elements of what the particular form wants to explore. Marrying the two aspects helps to realize what can be done within a show. And just as important, if not more, is that on any given evening you need to ...

KNOW *THIS* SHOW

At some point in a show, even in a form you've done hundreds of times, the show will start to let you know what it wants, how it is seeking to be different than every other Harold, Deconstruction or Switch ever done. Only by paying attention to what has been done (on purpose or accidentally) can you understand what is required of you at the moment. Notice how the sequence of the scenes makes you feel, how all the elements have conspired to create a unique evening, of which you are a small part—can I understand what is required of me at this moment? This is this show. This is not another show. This one's different. It is probably not what you thought it would be or where it would go. But this is the show you are in. Moreover, if you can hear it, it's telling you what to do next. So listen to what the show is asking for. It's not about what you want it to be. The performer's will must not be stronger than the show's.

Very soon after beginning any form of show, we can start the process of listening to what our show wants. If a Harold opening is transformational, we can bring that into the show. If the first three scenes feel like 1950s filmstrips, we should pay attention to that. If the show presents large group images, epic scale, bold, Spartacus-like declarations, we can lean into that. Maybe every time we see a particular character, we get a sneaking sense that he is a little melancholy or mischievous, so we can allow ourselves to be influenced by that. Remember, we are not writing the show; we are observing and participating in it.

What does this show need from me? The only way to know is to pay close attention to everything. This show may be asking for me to walk out with a powerful, high-tempo initiation. This show could need me to sing the second verse of a ballad. It may need me to deliver a heartfelt monologue downstage center. I'm convinced that I am capable of doing all these things as I walk out to do them. I can do them because they need doing.

Or it may not be a big thing that's being asked of me. It can be something as simple as "This scene needs to be edited," so I should edit it. We all know that feeling. When you're watching a scene and you get the impulse to edit, maybe your foot even moves forward. But then you stop that impulse because you don't really have anything to say. *Not your job.* Your foot was right. Your brain was wrong. All scenes are edited because they need to be edited at that moment. The scene editor's job is primarily to end the previous scene, without regard to whether or not he has an idea for the next scene. We were taught that editing scenes is another way of looking out for each other. Help a brother/sister out, man—that's the main task.

> **Your foot was right. Your brain was wrong.**

EMOTIONAL POINT OF VIEW

In *TJ & Dave*, a character's emotional state is often arrived at gradually as the scene is revealed. However, we find it most useful to funnel everything—from audience suggestions to developing relationships with our scene partner— through an emotional point of view.

This approach gives us a strong, sustainable foundation from which we can view our partner and the world. It's hard to do a five-minute scene about the action of detailing one's Camaro, but we could probably improvise *forever* as a guy whose whole damn life is wrapped up in his car. More importantly, an internalized point of view lets our partners know who we are and gives them something to react to. In this way, it's self-supporting and a helpful state to work in for us both.

> **An internalized point of view lets our partners know who we are and gives them something to react to.**

An emotional point of view is different than an intellectual point of view. A player could enter a scene with a point of view, but if there isn't an emotion attached to it, then there isn't a mode of behavior to follow or an emotion to connect them to their partners. For instance, let's say our intellectual point of view is that the world is run by corporate giants. That would be fine for some social or political satire, but we probably wouldn't want to do a whole scene based only on this view. That point of view does not help to serve or inform the relationship. What's more important is how we *feel* about the world being run by corporate giants.

Say we're doing a scene set in a quaint little diner, and the waitress is standing in front of us. Since our belief is that the world is run by corporate giants, we think, "How does that make us *feel* here in the diner?" Let's say that view makes us feel displeased with the state of the world and we want to root for mom-and-pop shops. We can allow that viewpoint to inform our physicality, our voice, our environment, and how we feel about our partner. So even as we look around that diner, the sign "Enjoy Coca-Cola" makes us a little upset. This emotional point of view also causes us to sit differently because we would like to appear as if we're just homespun kind of guys. Plus, the language we choose could be down-home, folksy in nature. So if the waitress asks us, "What ya' in the mood for, hon?" then we have a point of reference as someone who is rooting for mom and pops while we're pondering what to order. We would look to see if they had a special from a local farmer, see what's in season, what's homemade, a fresh pie. And more importantly we want to bring that point of view to the relationship. We would want to find out about the waitress, how she grew up, see her as an individual in a real "Power to the people!" kind of way. Maybe we would be even more interested in her if she was from this little town. Maybe we would settle down in this quaint town, and try to make a go of it as gentlemen farmers.

> **An emotional point of view gives us a lens that we can use to look at the entire world.**

We don't have to be heavy handed with our emotional angle. We can be specific in our perspective without being obvious and overly narrative. We don't have to come straight out and say, "I'm not going to order Coke because that was made by a global conglomerate and I want to support the little people." Instead, we can say that very same idea in a more natural fashion. "I sure would love to try somethin' from 'round here" gets the same intent across. We're not terribly worried if the audience understands that we're all about grassroots organizations. Even our scene partner doesn't need to know our motivation is being against big corporate giants. All our scene partner needs to do is merely respond to the line, "I sure would love somethin' from 'round here." She is not responsible for figuring out our motivation; she's just got to respond to what she hears, however she would. Improvisation is not a guessing game. It's a scene. As long as we know where we're coming from and stay open to being affected by our partner, then we've got a shot.

Let's change the one word "corporate" to "fairy tale." And now our point of view is the world is run by fairy tale giants. We still go through the same process. We still think, "Okay, how does that make us *feel*? It makes us feel scared because we are small, so we want to get larger." So we might sit bigger in our chairs. If we were at the same diner counter, perhaps we'd try to spread wide, take up another stool, because we want to seem large and not a convenient target for an ogre lumbering by. We would speak in a way that would infer a greater size. And if the waitress asked that same question, "What ya' in the mood for, hon?" we are going to look at the menu for the biggest, most protein-filled and carb-loaded things they have, like The Hungry Man's Special. And we'll order three entrées rather than just one. When we speak to the waitress, we would try to seem more imposing and seek to dominate a little more because we want to portray our strength in the same way we'd want to seem bigger if we encountered a bear or a lion in the wild. No matter what world we're in, an emotional point of view gives us a lens that we can use to look at the entire world.

> **As long as we know where we're coming from and stay open to being affected by our partner, then we've got a shot.**

AUDIENCE SUGGESTIONS

This approach can be applied to how we take an audience suggestion, how we use source material (like a monologue in a monologue deconstruction), and how we initiate a scene. We try to take a piece of information and distill that down to an emotional point of view. You can usually translate an audience suggestion into an emotional point of view in order to attach a feeling to it that allows you to play from an internal base rather than merely from an external activity.

When getting a suggestion, it first needs to be honored in a way that would be recognizable to a first-time viewer of improvisation, so there is a bit of transparency there. But we can still allow the suggestion to affect us emotionally in a way that might not be obvious to the audience (which is fine, because this approach is something we're doing for ourselves, not for them). So let's imagine an audience member calls out the suggestion "Christmas tree." We can help ourselves out by resisting the immediate impulse just to head over to put an ornament on a Christmas tree, and instead, add to that action some feelings or emotions we associate with Christmas tree or Christmas or decorating a tree. We might think about stuff like, "Is it the most wonderful time of the year? Does the over-commercialization of Christmas rankle us? Do we miss someone whom we don't get to celebrate Christmas with anymore? Is our favorite part the not knowing what's under the tree?" This way, we'll be more personally equipped and of more use to a partner if we take a half-second to associate the action with a viewpoint.

A suggestion of "Christmas tree" might prompt us to become someone who's always looking for what their partner says to be a gift, to be a compliment, a personally wrapped present just for us. So if our scene partner says, "It's getting late," we think, "Oh my God! It's so great that she thought of me! We probably do need to go to sleep." This way, we have a solid emotional base from which to move out into any possible direction this scene might take us. Or else maybe the suggestion of "Christmas tree" makes us think of grandparents who passed away and we don't get to see them at Christmas anymore. So if our partner says, "It's getting late," we might respond, "Yeah, we'll all be dead soon." And then we take it from there, from one moment to another.

Regardless of what the suggestion may be or what type of structure we're using, the goal is still to do a great scene. So why not let that suggestion put us in a place where we feel most equipped to do a great scene? Having an emotional point of view to operate from can do that. We'll still put a Christmas tree in the scene, which will satisfy the overt need to use that suggestion. But to internalize and be informed by an emotion often makes us most comfortable and, therefore, of most use to our partner.

STARTING A SCENE

Let's continue with the Christmas tree example, and let's say that we miss our grandparents who aren't here anymore. Since it's the first second of the scene, we don't know where we are and who our scene partner is to us yet— we really don't know a thing. But we can know what internalized viewpoint the suggestion inspires in us. In this case, "Christmas tree" made us think of being sad that our grandparents aren't here anymore to celebrate with us. So the first line of the scene simply could be a gloomy "Well ... there's fewer of us this time."

Ideally, what is most important is not even those words but that we give our partner a heads-up about our emotional state. So we're going to put it in our body and our face and look to our partner to see what they are doing. If our partner speaks first, we still can come into the scene knowing that we're down in the mouth and our grandparents are dead and we miss them. So whatever our partner says is going through that filter. If neither of us say anything and our location is revealed first—if we find ourselves at a Christmas tree farm—we can look to see how this place is designed to make us sad, always playing through those feelings and answering those questions of "What does this make me think of?" or "What does this make me feel?"

If we enter a scene with an intellectual point of view, i.e., a lot of facts about a situation, we are almost certain to be in conflict with the facts our partner has secreted in his mind. But to come in with an emotional point of view means that I cannot disagree with any emotional point of view that my partner may have.

With first lines, we try to assume our partner knows what we're talking about even if they don't. That way, we don't fall into the trap of providing narrative garbage at the top of the scene. As each moment is revealed, it becomes true. If all goes well, we'll develop the scene one moment at a time, and soon enough we'll all know what's going on.

MAINTAINING POINT OF VIEW

Once established, that emotional point of view needs to be honored, even if it changes. Though facts can't be changed once they've been established— that table cannot vanish, my sister cannot suddenly become a stranger—our emotional point of view is more dynamic. If you think of it musically, your emotional point of view is that initial bass beat. Then, over the course of the piece, the musicians might inspire each other. The horn comes in and adds to that bass beat. Your point of view will be affected by your partner. Your sound will be altered by its mingling with your partner's sound. Listen to how *Ode to Joy* starts out. It goes to a lot of different places, but you never feel like you've lost where it began. And when that original melody returns at the end after you've gone on this trip, and you recognize it: "Ah! That's the guy I met first! He's still there!" As an improviser, it's our job to grab that point of view but realize that it's not a static bar. It never goes away, though it can move and fluctuate. And if our partner—God bless him—gives us enough reasons to be almost an entirely different person by the end, then that partner did one helluva job. They gave me a lot of good reasons to have done this 180°.

You'll watch someone go through any amount and size of change if it's done for a believable reason. If someone makes a change for any reason you don't believe, you've just seen someone give up on their choice. We're not supposed to be impenetrable and immutable in our work. Our viewpoint is supposed to be acted upon, molded as it goes. And given good reason, we should change as is warranted by what was said or done or whatever moment has passed.

This is what being vulnerable in improvisation is really about. People sometimes misunderstand what it means to "play vulnerable." We take it to mean weak or needy, low status or fragile. It just means not invulnerable. If we are vulnerable, we can be penetrated. We can be acted upon. Performing with more vulnerability is trying to be impressionable or open or willing to change, which can be done whether we're playing a hard-ass drill instructor or a tender kindergarten teacher. It's a fun way to play because we get to be in a constant place of reaction.

IN CONVERSATION:
Mastering, Breaking, and Listening to Your Show

PAM: What do you mean by "Play inside the form and get it, so you can master it and break it right"?

TJ: Do the Harold a few hundred times before you decide to jump off. Understand it from the inside, from the box being rigid, before you decide to mutate it, so that you know how and why you want to adapt it. Before you try to figure out what's wrong with it, first figure out what's right with it, and then make an informed choice to do something different.

PAM: I want to understand that idea of your show talking back to you.

TJ: Once you understand what a show is trying to do, how it moves ... once you get to a level of "expertise," then you're free to listen to your show. You can set out to do a straight Harold, but then, "Wait a minute. Through some of the ideas that came up in the opening and some of the things that came out during the three scenes and some of the revelations within that group game, this show is telling us it wants us to do a set of second beats where everyone takes a turn playing the lady we met called Janet." Or this *Armando* is saying that because of the ideas that have been out there, this second act is supposed to be the first act backwards. Based on stuff that's going on, a show is telling us that it wants to be a certain way. Each show has the potential to be unique within this form because it's taken on its own life now. We've done both the homework and the work within this show to be able to listen and follow it now.

PAM: So you're saying a performer needs some flexibility in order for the show to exert its will?

TJ: The performer's will can't be stronger than the show's will. And that's why those early points in learning a form are important—understanding what your form says it wants to explore, working within the construct of this form over and over again—so that you've done all the time in the batting cage or in the gym, so that you can trust now to listen back to it and help it do what it wants to do.

> **The performer's will can't be stronger than the show's will.**

PAM: I imagine that would require a pretty special group dynamic or at least a respect for each other, the form, and the art form.

TJ: Yeah, I think it's respect for the form and the trust that it wants to live, and now that's our job to keep it alive. It's tough to explain. In *J. T.S. Brown*, it feels like, "God, this thing has taken over, and now all we have to do is feed it." For a while, a baby eats whatever you give it. But after you've done your best to nourish it and tried to be a good parent and made a home for this child, this show, it starts to tell you, "Oh, I like this. I want to do this." And then at that point, once your show starts to talk back to you like that, you do your best to fulfill those desires and needs. What it wants. But you had to do all those things before to get yourself in a position where you can do that.

PAM: Right. You have to walk before you can dance.

TJ: Yes. And be confident enough in yourself that your ego is not a part of it anymore. You're just pleasantly allowed to be in service to this thing that is your show now. You are beautiful when you are free, and you are most free when you're of service to the scene, to the show, and to the moment.

> **You are beautiful when you are free, and you are most free when you're of service to the scene, to the show, and to the moment.**

PAM: That must be such a wonderful transition as a performer.

TJ: It's awesome. It feels sooo good. In a way, it's counter-intuitive that it should feel as good as it does because it's like, "Well, it's not even my will anymore. Now I'm just in service to this *thing*? I just gotta do this job that the show wants me to do?" But it feels so freeing to be in servitude to a show.

PAM: I really think inanimate objects feel their best when they are serving their purpose. Like a sock is much happier being a sock on your foot than in your laundry basket.

TJ: When a teapot is serving tea, it feels right at home?

PAM: Yes, exactly. And it's sad sitting on a shelf being unused.

TJ: Or being used as a change bin?

PAM: Well, maybe that particular teapot is an outlier? Maybe being a change bin is its true purpose in life?

TJ: And you can't fill it with change until you understand what it does as itself.

PAM: That's right. It has to know what it feels like to be a teapot before it knows it's happy being a change bin.

TJ: In 2004, I worked with a group called *The Outsiders* that came up with a form based on repetition we called The Fibonacci. Do you know what the Fibonacci Sequence is?

PAM: Yes, I do. 0, 1, 1, 2, 3, 5 ... where each number is the sum of the previous two.

TJ: So we'd do Scene A, and then Scene B. And then we would do Scene A again but affected by something that happened in Scene B. Then we'd do Scene B again affected by the second beat of Scene A. Then inspired by what happened, we'd do Scene C. Then we would do Scene A again, affected by that C scene, then we'd do Scene B again affected by the third run of Scene A. Scene C would come back again affected by the second showing of Scene B. And those would inspire a Scene D. Scene A would come again for the fourth time, affected by Scene B. B would come for the third time affected by the fourth time of Scene A ... do you see the structure?

PAM: I do. You're constantly being informed by the previous scene.

TJ: Exactly. You know how we always talk about the idea that failure is inherent within improvisation, so it's just a given that we will mess it up? We sought to explore that place because we definitely would mess it up in this form. It's impossible. We would get to a point in the sequence where we just couldn't remember whether we're supposed to be doing Scene B or C or the fifth iteration of A, so the real joy of it is what happens when we mess it up. Because I might have thought we were doing the fifth time of Scene A, Mark thought we were going back into Scene B, and now what is it we're doing? The fifth A? The fourth B? Is it an actual over-the-board E scene? And what do we do after that? Do we do Scene B or C or go back and try to do A again? The real joy of that show didn't happen until two-thirds of the way through, where we got confused, by design and despite our best efforts, and we were in the realm of the impossible. We were trying our best, but what the hell was next?

PAM: You're accessing a place of pure creativity.

TJ: A freeing place of failure and loss. We wanted to get to pure exploration through our most honest efforts to do it right, knowing that we couldn't, and that failure would come and get us at some point.

PART SIX

CONCLUSIONS AND ACKNOWLEDGEMENTS

21

OUR BETTER HALVES

> Our virtues and our failings are inseparable, like force and matter.
> When they separate, man is no more.
>
> *– Nikola Tesla*

———————————

Hanging out with TJ and David can be a remarkable experience where different planes of communication are occurring simultaneously. In addition to the regular, out loud plane of words and body language, there is a silent, invisible plane that exists only between them. You get the sense that more is being said—and it's probably funny and smart and irreverent. You can only guess. It's like twinspeak. You'll never be on their secret channel ... and that's okay. What is clear between TJ and David is the sense that these two men share a profound respect and affection for each other.

Near the beginning of the book, TJ and David reflected on what makes a good stage partner. Over the course of writing that chapter, they separately wrote about what makes the other an exceptional partner onstage. Here's what they had to say:

DAVID SPEAKS ON TJ AS A PARTNER

Not everything is a gift.

I believe that if I do less than my best onstage, somebody should beat the shit out of me. And I can't do my best unless others around me are better than I am. To me, TJ is that person with whom I can lay it all on the line, try my best, and push myself to the limits of (and perhaps beyond) my abilities. He's a great improviser, so I have to keep up or get left in the dust. We don't do the same things, though we seem to have a similar interest in seeing what happens if we actually improvise this way. We have a strange ability to communicate because we are both paying attention. This kind of experiment requires that. I'm really lucky to have stumbled onto TJ.

It is necessary to know that our partners will not sell us out, that we can try things and not be hung out to dry. There has to be that trust in place so that we can dare to be foolish (or beautiful) without worry that we are doing it alone. You simply will not risk being a fool if your partner stands apart from you and declares, "God, what a fool you are." Well, you're not likely to do it more than once anyway. (Or you're an idiot.)

On the other side of that is the great joy of being able to improvise with someone you can trust to handle your giving your best. I enjoy having an improvising partner who is able to contend with anything I have for him and who is confident that he can do the same. Not only am I confident TJ will take care of me, I also am confident TJ can take care of himself, that I need not treat him with kid gloves. I don't have to worry he won't be able to handle my "searing intellect" or my unbridled wrath. I don't have to worry about him hurting me or me hurting him. I don't have any constraints on myself because I'm free to do anything because of his ability. Because of him, I don't have to be afraid to try my best. And therefore, we can give one another our very best. That is a gift ... to give someone your best.

TJ'S TAKE

I didn't get to paint with Cezanne or write with Faulkner, but I get to play with Dave, who made me want to do the work in the first place ... to be able to play with the folks that you watched from way in the back, who inspired you to try this as a lifestyle, is a rare privilege.

– TJ Jagodowski
(excerpted from Chicago Improv Festival interview,
conducted after the first time TJ and David shared a stage,
May 2001)

It is not easy to describe what makes David a good scene partner, because he is truly unique and, by definition, incomparable. Anyone who has met him will agree there is simply no one like him. He vibrates on a higher plane, and we were all surprised he didn't vanish when the Mayan calendar ran out.

The way David pays attention is something to behold. He has the focus of a microscope, but the breadth of a telescope. I've never met anyone who listens like he does. It is an amazingly active thing to watch him hear you. It's equally warming to know that you are being that purposefully taken in. The care he puts into it makes you feel like you're worth being cared about. When we first started working together, I remember equating David's attention to being welcomed into a lantern light. It was cozy and private. I knew people were there, observing, but it felt very intimate. I could and can still give the slightest indication as to what I'm feeling or thinking, and I know it will be perceived and read by him. That is an intensely freeing way to play.

Especially in the first year we played together, I was scared shitless all the time. (Truth is, I get scared shitless most of the time.) And so was Dave. The difference was, I hated that feeling while he loved it. He loved it because it was his body telling him that this is worth doing.

David is very unforgiving of himself as an improviser. After the sheer man-hours he has logged onstage, there could be a temptation to cut himself some slack, but he doesn't. And this high level of desiring excellence is not from show to show, but from second to second. In holding these standards for himself, he makes me want to hold myself to the same. He simply makes me better. I've never improvised better than I have with David, and that is entirely because of him.

Dave is curious by nature, so he is smart. He is fearless in life, so he is interesting. He understands sadness, so he is funny. He has his demons, so he is forgiving. He gives and needs in equal portion, so he is a partner. And because there is no one like him, they had to come up with other words to describe him. The words they came up with were David Pasquesi.

IN CONVERSATION:

MAGIC, THE FUTURE, AND THE BEST IMPROVISER IN THE WORLD

Be where you are; otherwise you will miss your life.

— Buddha

In this closing conversation, we widen our scope to tackle more sweeping and less tangible topics: the best that improvisation can be; moments of magic onstage; hopes for the future of improvisation; even humility. Plus, we throw in baseball, world domination, and other personal pleasures.

PAM: You once told me that improvisation is different than regular life. It's better. That your brains work differently in that state, and you never feel alone. That it's proof that something beyond yourselves is being revealed. Can you tell me more about how you internally experience that magical feeling of "Harold being in the room"?

DAVID: It feels like you are a passenger being carried along as well as an active, present participant. It's pretty great.

This guy named Mihaly Csikszentmihalyi wrote a book called *FLOW: The Psychology of Optimal Experience* that my wife turned me on to. That's what I think it is, one of those optimal experiences.

TJ: I was thinking about it last night before I heard David's answer, and mine was the same almost word for word. You're a participant, but you're also an observer. It's an odd, wonderful sort of feel. And now that you mention *Flow*, it's a bit like there is a song that is always playing or there's a poem that's always being read, but when that extra thing happens—when Harold visits—you hear it. For this little bit of time, you're so connected to another person or a group of people that you're able to hear this music that's always there just beyond your sense and it seems to help determine what it is that you're supposed to do next. And now everyone is hearing it.

PAM: Have you ever felt that way off the stage?

DAVID: Not that I recall ... not without psychedelics.

TJ: I think the closest that I feel is either being in love or something in nature where, again, you're like a participant but you're also an observer. And it's something big. And there's this excited piece to it.

PAM: Has there ever been a sport or a musical instrument that made you feel that way?

DAVID: Maybe something like rock climbing, where you have to be completely involved. I think that seems to be one of the criteria that I have, to be completely involved in this right here and right now. And I guess there is also fear involved, in both improvisation and rock climbing. One of them is actual physical danger and the other is the fear of humiliation.

TJ: I would say the sport I got best at was baseball, and there would be moments where I would feel this excited high, but it was more alone. Just by myself at the plate. In improvisation, the feeling of doing it with at least one other person, if not seven or eight more people, is so much more exciting.

DAVID: I think improvisation is unique in that we're all doing it. It's not just happening to one person.

PAM: Except for falling in love, which involves other people ... ideally.

DAVID: Ideally, yeah. But there are a billion stories about unrequited love. It's still love.

PAM: That's true. The loneliest love of all.

TJ: Dave right now is practicing one of those lonely forms of love. Right, David?

DAVID: I'm not practicing. I'm pretty good! You might say I'm a master.

PAM: Aside from various forms of love, what are your hopes for the future of improvisation?

TJ: My hope is that it keeps on growing in every direction and getting better in every way.

DAVID: Yeah, and I don't care about the growing, but I think the getting better is great. Improvisation is being more widely spread, certainly. The great thing about it is that audiences aren't as afraid of it or immediately dismissive of it. Because not that long ago, improvisers could not get audiences at legitimate theaters.

TJ: I know I found improvisation at the right time for me, but I wish it happened more often in places like Western Massachusetts. Outside of Pam's group or us going up at the Deuce *[aka the World War Two Club, a bar/banquet hall in Northampton]*, I don't know how often Western Massachusetts has it outside a college campus. I would love to have seen it as a younger man.

PAM: You're saying that one of your hopes is that it's more accessible? That more kids can be turned on to it, so they can start to take a path of their own?

TJ: I don't even know if it's just kids. I think the more people try, the greater the chances for more good improvisation. There may be some phenomenal kid in rural Kansas who just doesn't know about it. Or an adult in the Dakotas.

PAM: It's true. It's definitely moving in that direction. Several high schools in my area have improvisation troupes.

TJ: Yeah, and I'm a little torn about it because I don't know when people should start improvising. I waver on that perhaps because of the few folks I have met who came to improvisation very young and thought they knew all there was to know by the time they were twenty. I think for improvisation to have its full force, it needs players to have a grasp on emotional maturity. And certainly age doesn't guarantee that, but it improves the chances. It's not that there isn't value to it at every age—the tenets of improvisation should make for a lovely blueprint for good living—but young folks' improvisation, even at its best, is a bit like watching a piano savant. They may play the piece perfectly, yet they lack the life experience to translate the notes to feelings.

DAVID: I am so fortunate that I was introduced to improvisation through Judy Morgan, a great teacher, a lover of improvisation, and a great improviser. I imagine a lot of folks don't have as good an introduction.

TJ: When I say I want it to keep growing in all different directions, I want more excellent, patient, two-person scene work ... and I want more awesome lunacy ... and I want more great sketches that come from improvising a scene over and over again. I want it to move in all directions and get better in all directions.

DAVID: I just want to differentiate between "more" and "good." More is not necessarily good. In talking about the future of improvisation, my wish isn't just to have a lot of it, but that there is good improvisation. More improvisation with *integrity* is what I'm wishing for, I guess.

TJ: It's tough to say what it is exactly, but we just want it to be frickin' awesome. Anything at its best is really great to see.

DAVID: Right. No matter what form it takes.

TJ: Yeah!

PAM: Do you have any goals, hopes, or dreams for your show? Anything you haven't done yet that you'd like to try out?

TJ: I think we're still looking forward to every show we haven't done yet or tried out.

DAVID: Yes, one of the goals is to do it right, I suppose.

PAM: If your wildest fantasies came true for your life in improvisation, what would that look like?

DAVID: World domination.

TJ: I think I've been living my dream improv life. I have a lot of opportunities to play in a bunch of the theaters I respect with people I really enjoy, the gem of which is on Wednesdays with David. It's pretty dreamy to be a part of the city where I think it's done the best.

DAVID: I have to say that I'm pretty happy with what I get to do as well. That we get to explore this thing a bunch ...

TJ: ... without anyone ever telling us we could or could not do something.

DAVID: A lot of that is Charna [Halpern]. From the beginning, she's just let us do whatever we wanted to do, and that's pretty great. I'm not sure we'd be so trusting of people like us.

PAM: What do mean, "people like us"?

DAVID: Improvisers.

PAM: You see yourself as plain, ol' improvisers?

TJ: That's what we are. We are improvisers.

PAM: I guess we've stumbled on a chance here to address this dynamic about the place of humbleness in improvisation. Some people are surprised at your humility. Some people think that it's misplaced. Some people really love it. But in general, people seem perplexed by it because they think you guys are ... well ... awesome.

DAVID: That's awful nice of them.

TJ: I think we've been doing it a long time, and I think we've gotten pretty good at it. But I also would say that the more you understand about it—and this applies to any pursuit—you realize things like masters don't exist. It's like that Pablo Casals quote we referred to a while ago.

PAM: That he was still practicing five hours a day at the age of 95 because he thought he was "finally making some progress."

TJ: Yeah. I watch a bunch of those cooking shows, and it's Jacques Pepin and Wolfgang Puck, but it's just about letting the food talk. Let an onion be its delicious self. We are hoping to be in the show where improvisation speaks for itself. I think the more you study anything, the more you realize you don't know shit yet. And all it's going to take is the rest of your life to start knowing something about it.

PAM: Do you think this humble nature is a necessary component of improvisation?

> The more you study anything, the more you realize you don't know shit yet. And all it's going to take is the rest of your life to start knowing something about it.

DAVID: I don't think we view it as a humble nature ...

TJ: ... it's what improvisation says. It's not a secret. They tell you from the beginning that your partner is the bigger thing. That the show is the bigger thing. That the moment is the bigger thing. And I don't know if improvisers just pass over that or don't keep that in the hopper as to what we should be thinking all the time, but it says it right from the start. I don't know that humility is the word for it. But service is inherent. That you are less important than something and someone else is Day One.

PAM: To play devil's advocate, there are groups that I look up to as benchmarks, goals to aim for. And when I look as high and far as I can see, your show is at the top. *For me.* So what is it you're aiming for? Does that show even exist?

TJ: We aim for our best show. We don't compare our show to other shows. We compare our show to our ideal show. And we know on any given night how far away our show is from what we want our show to be.

> That's the thing that excites me the most when I'm watching improvisation—people who are committed to what's going on right now.

DAVID: And I think other people's shows aren't trying to be our show. When I go and watch other people who are really good and work really well together, what I notice and what I steal from them is oftentimes how committed the person was in the moment. That's the thing that excites me the most when

I'm watching improvisation—people who are committed to what's going on right now, and they sweep me along with them.

PAM: Is that what makes the best improviser, someone who is deeply committed?

TJ: If we want to say there's a title of "Best Improviser in the World," it should be handed out half-second by half-second. Whoever in the globe at that moment is performing most honestly, most selflessly, most free, that's the best improviser in the world. Then in the next second, someone is going to be doing it better than anyone else in the world. On any given night, that's a different person. In any given second, that's a different person.

PAM: I wanna get me a piece of that trophy.

TJ: You may have at some point been the best improviser in the world, Pam.

DAVID: Yeah, you may already have it.

PAM: There aren't that many people improvising in China yet, so if I improvise at an off-hour when only Chinese people are awake, I'd have a better shot ...

TJ: Yeah, but even if only 0.5% of China is improvising, you're screwed.

PAM: That's true!

TJ: And then the Pakistanis will start improvising just to defy the Indians, and then ... oh boy...

PAM: Oh boy. Well, I've been asking you questions for over a year. My last question is do you have any questions for me?

DAVID: Did you learn anything from this? Did it directly affect the way you improvise?

PAM: Absolutely. Without a doubt. Well, we'll see how often I get to touch the trophy. But as far as this approach goes, the biggest challenge is finding people who are interested in doing it.

DAVID: Yup. When you were asking about improvisation and our hopes ... I really do feel lucky to be doing it with TJ, and we both seem interested in trying to find out this thing together.

PAM: I would love to find somebody who could help guide me to get me there more and not to tempt me into less useful habits. But over our time working together, I think I've definitely become a better improviser. I hope so.

DAVID: That's the way it started too for me. We didn't know what a Harold was. We had never seen one. It's the same thing.

PAM: Absolutely.

DAVID: So, clearly, you don't need to have someone show you.

PAM: Yeah. I guess I just need to take the next step.

22

CONCLUSIONS AND ACKNOWLEDGEMENTS

TJ JAGODOWSKI

There is so much I don't know. Of all the things in the world I should have learned, I probably know the most about improvisation and I know almost nothing. But I am, in most ways, because of improvisation, understanding a bit more about myself. And if feelings can be fact, then I can say I know this thing for sure: I am so very grateful for improvisation.

Improvisation has given me nearly everything I have. It gave me a sense of who I am. It introduced me to my greatest friends. It has thrilled and educated me. It brought me to the woman I love. It has given me an adult life filled with laughter. It earned me a living. It has shown me the country. And though it didn't give me my family, it does give us occasions to all be together and spend a night in each other's company.

I gave myself to improvisation, and it gave me back a better me.

That's one of my favorite things about improvisation: All it wants is you. It says you've done all the homework needed to be good at it. You stayed alive to 'til now. And along the way, you've felt and learned. You've talked to people. You've thought the most lovely and atrocious stuff imaginable. And improvisation gives you a place for it all. Brings you to it. Those oddities and eccentricities. Your most sensitive self. Your highest aspiration and basest impulse have their arena. Improvisation wants all of you. Every angelic height and dusty corner. It says you don't have to hide any part of you anymore.

It only wants your whole soul. But that's all. It only wants everything.

TJ WOULD LIKE TO THANK …

These thank-yous and appreciations are in particular and exact order as pertains to the importance of the persons or groups mentioned. It is an all-inclusive list. Any omissions are purposeful and meant to be taken personally.

The people who invented bread, awesome job; my mom and dad, I am literally nothing without you; Beth for joy and love and walks and Bones; my brothers Todd and Troy, being one of three boys felt very right in the world; Nan and Pop, at 43, I still have grandparents that laugh and live and could beat me in a fight; Babcie and Dziadziu, you are missed; my Uncles Gary and Jamey and George, the first funny people in my life because when you're little your folks aren't allowed to be funny; Di, Lauren, James, Lil' Gary, Sean, the rest of my lovely twisted kind hard gracefulness and gracelessful amazing family, you are home and many of you will end up in homes.

Sean "The Kid" Keane, his family up and down, Matt Collamore, Todd Fallon, Jim Athas (the best coach I ever had), Holyoke Catholic High, 49 Elmwood Ave and the good people of Holyoke, Massachusetts. The Boston Red Sox. Jeff Colburn, Brian Dubina, Jason Lycette, Pedro Martinez, Josh Mann, Jason Zahn, Ben Greene, Marcus Russell, Stanley Morgan, Mosi Tatupu and Stevie B. Dean Thomas Michael O'Shea, my other coach and friend. Jack McBrayer, Michael Patrick O'Brien and Billy Bungeroth; killers all and best friends in no uncertain terms. Peter Grosz who does all the hard work and makes every time a pleasure. Kevin Dorff, my mentor and mate, who taught me as much about living honorably as performing and invited me to the round table both Arthurian and Algonquin. The moon for showing up every night for work. Lisa Haleski Masseur for opening the door to my life. Paul Grondo who deserves the world. Peaches, the man and the fruit. Mick Napier for things innumerable, deep things like how to be helpful, how to behave toward people, how to be true to oneself. Scott Adsit and Steph Weir for handling my idolizing with grace. John Lutz, Alex Fendrich, Kevin McHale, Andy St. Clair, Dan Bakkedahl, sitting on a porch, Suzie Gillan, Jake Schneider, Bobby Orr, Carl Yastrzemski, Craig Cackowski, Peter Gwinn, Bob Dassie, Case Clay, Joe Bill and casinos. Josie and Mabel for being little, quiet and furry. Chewbacca for being big, quiet and furry. Matt Cullison for years of laughing and companionship. Tony DeSantis, Jim Sullivan, Paul Howe and Kevin McGeehan for making houses homes. The G.O.C. and Holyoke Youth Baseball.

Charna Halpern, The Captain and The Truth Paul Pierce, Kelly Leonard, Beth Kligerman, Larry Bird, Andrew Alexander, Joyce Sloane, Bernie Sahlins, Sheldon Patinkin, Jen Estlin, the trivia website Sporcle, Dexter Bullard, Don

DePollo, Zdeno Chara, Michael Gellman, a great book, Norm Holly, Martin deMaat. Linda Jack, Mickey Grossman, Dustin Pedroia, Suzie Gardiner, Linda Bernasconi. Scott Morfee, Tom Wirtshafter, the staff at The Barrow, pizza. Al Samuels, Nomar Garciaparra, Abby Sher, Pam Klier, Andy Cobb, Kristin Ford, Holly Walker, early years Jason Varitek, Dave Pompeii, Klaus Schuller, TJ Shanoff. A nice cup of joe, Rich Talarico, WEEI, Susan Messing, Tami Sagher. Sam Albert, Keegan-Michael Key, butternut squash, Josh Funk. Jim Zulevic, Tom Brady, Tina Fey, Rachel Dratch, Horatio Sanz, Matt Dwyer, Rebeccah Sohn, Jerry Minor and Carlton Fisk.

IO, The Second City, Mighty Mighty BlueCo., the CTA Brown Line, The Annoyance, Robert Parish, Carl and the Passions, ChicagoLand, TNT, Misled, 99% Invisible, Georgia Pacific, Armando Diaz (show and man), Bucket, The Royal Tennenbaums, JTS Brown, going for walks, The Outsiders, The Reckoning, Atlantis, Almost Atlanta, Baker and Nosh, Knight and Day, Ted Williams.

Matt Higbee, Harrison George, RadioLab, Ike Reilly and F. Tyler Burnet for making the show the show.

Pam, without whom there for sure would be no book, J.M. Pasquesi who fixed the book, and David, without whom there would have been nothing to make a book about.

And the City of Chicago, a city in a garden where amazingly beautiful things grow.

DAVID PASQUESI

> This is this. This ain't something else. This is this.
> — *Robert DeNiro as Michael Vronsky in The Deer Hunter*

It dawns on me that I have been living this particular life all along. Not another life. This one. This life that I have not designed or planned. In fact, I would probably have planned a different one had I the opportunity, ability, or gumption. This whole thing is improvisation.

I have been improvising for this long because I have been improvising for this long. And I'm still trying to do the same things I started out trying to do over thirty years ago with Del Close and those guys at Crosscurrents.

I like to think that TJ and I are continuing the "kind of stuff" that Del asked me to remember to keep doing in his last days. And I also like to think, he wouldn't yell at me if he saw us.

DAVID WOULD LIKE TO THANK ...

I'd like to thank my wife and our editor/publisher Joan Marie Pasquesi, and my sons, Giancarlo and Luca Pasquesi. TJ Jagodowski. Pam Victor, without whom we would not have undertaken this book. Pat, Ted, Tommy, and Johnny Pasquesi, and My Aunt Connie.

Friends and influences, Del Close, Charna Halpern, Joel Murray, Bernie Sahlins, everybody I've ever worked with. Judy Morgan, Fred Kaz, Jeff Sweet, David Shepherd, Alex Karpovsky, Ike Reilly, everyone I admire.

Scott Morfee and Tom Wirtshafter of the Barrow Street Theatre, our home in New York. Jane Borden, Matt Love, David Yazbek for their support and friendship.

Baron's Barracudas, Joel Murray, Chris Barnes, Howard Johnson, Mark Beltzman, Honor Finnegan, J.J. Jones, John Judd, Steven Dale Burrows, Brian E. Crane, Judy Neilsen, Bill Russell. Richard Kind, Brian Doyle-Murray, Harold Ramis, Joyce Sloane, Andrew Alexander, Tracy Letts, Sue Gillan, Michael Shannon, Jeff Garlin, Emo Phillips, Tim Kazurinsky, Bobcat Goldthwait, David Cross, Paul Gilmartin, F. Tyler Burnett, Matt Higbee, and all the people who come to our shows and enjoy them or at least hold us accountable.

PAM VICTOR

I hadn't realized I'd been living in a dim world until improvisation came into my life and the lights flickered on. Gradually, all the dangling threads of my me-ness began to weave together in a surprisingly wondrous fashion as I realized that all my life had been a preparation for this moment. The first time TJ asked me (and the rest of the audience) to trust him and Dave, that light took on focus and detail. I suddenly saw all that improvisation could be. The journey from *TJ & Dave* fangirl to TJ and David's co-author has indelibly changed me into a better improviser, teacher, and maybe even human. Improvisation is the unreachable dream, defyingly complex in its simplicity, a lifelong search for an ease-fulness that burns much effort in its trail until it is extinguished.

PAM WOULD LIKE TO THANK ...

I'm a big fan of gratitude, so it's a pleasure to have a whole section to thank the some of many people who helped me do my part in getting his book into your hands (or paws, if you're a cat). Although "thank you" aren't big enough words to hold what I feel, it's all I gots, so here it goes. THANK YOU to ...

... David Pasquesi and TJ Jagodowski, first and foremost, whose performances never fail to make me believe in the Goddess of Improvisation. Your wholly unfounded faith and trust in me are among my most treasured and carefully protected possessions.

... my sisters in improvisation Laura Patrick, Christine Stevens, Moe McElligott, and Maile Shoul also known as The Ha-Ha's who show me every week how a true family is supposed to love, support, and tease each other. Remember that time we made Laura run out onstage to introduce us in the middle of that guy's story about his traumatic brain injury?

... my iO Summer Intensive 2012 team, Visibly Tight, and our brilliant teachers, who said, "Yes, and ..." to every one of my improviser dreams. Special thank-yous to Scott Hanada and Peter Kim for your friendship and support, to Stephanie Anderson for giving me that crucial talking-to at the Chicago Diner, and most of all to Stuart Scotten, who picked me up, dusted me off, and shoved me hard in the direction of TJ and David when I needed it most. Stuart, this book would not exist without your gentle bitchslaps and aggressively loving support, and for that I am eternally grateful.

... Charna Halpern for manifesting the best of improvisation in physical form and working tirelessly to maintain a home for geniuses, artists, and poets.

... my Boston mentor, Will Luera, and my Chicago mentor, Piero Procaccini, two of the biggest brains and hearts in improvisation.

... Susan Messing for holding my hand, patting me on the back, and slapping me upside the head at crucial moments of this adventure (depending on which I needed more). But most of all, thank you for being my role model of bravery.

... my "*Geeking Out with* ..." partners, who generously share your heads, hearts, and humor with me. All of you are my teachers, and I'm proud to have many of you as friends.

... Kim "Howard" Johnson and Michael Golding for being my go-to guys for improvisation history. Improvisation is like kindergarten in that you can walk up to someone and say, "Hi. We both love the same thing. Let's be friends." Thanks for meeting me by the tire swing and answering all my questions.

... the only two early test-readers who actually were able to finish the damn manuscript, Kerstin Warner Rao and Rose Dawson, for your patient reading and gentle feedback.

... to Jackie Victor, who knows all my secrets and for some unfathomable reason still loves me. Since before we were old enough to remember, I've loved you madly, admired you greatly, and been ridiculously proud of you. And that will never change, my dear cousinsisterfriend. Thanks for believing in me always.

... my children Jake and Sierra. You keep me grounded by mercilessly making fun of me at dinner every single night. I am so proud of both of you. The fact that you both also deeply love the arts makes me only prouder (and more worried about your future abilities to make rent). Thanks also to Jake for being such a great proofreader and to Sierra for always being willing to watch PG-13 rom-coms with me.

... and, most of all, to my ever-patient husband Jeff, the only person on this whole flippin' planet who unconditionally loves and supports me without bounds or end. Nobody else has sacrificed more for my career than you, and you've done so without complaint or expectations of retribution. If everyone had a spouse like mine, the world would be an infinitely better place. Thanks for not kicking me out of bed.

INDEX

We know it's over when the lights go out.

— TJ and Dave

ABOUT THE AUTHORS

TJ JAGODOWSKI

TJ Jagodowski began improvising in the mid-1990s and has learned, taught, performed or directed in just about all the improvisational theaters of Chicago. He has been at iO Chicago for twenty years, the Annoyance theater for fifteen, wrote and performed in two Second City reviews, and is co-founder and co-artistic director of The Mission Theater. His commercial, TV, and film credits include the Sonic ads, *Stranger than Fiction, Ice Harvest, The Great and Powerful Oz, Prison Break*, and *Get Hard*. Together with partner, David Pasquesi, TJ has performed the *TJ & Dave* show on many stages throughout the USA, Canada, and Europe. *(Photo courtesy of Robert Adam Mayer)*

DAVID PASQUESI

David has been improvising since the early 1980s. He studied with Del Close for years and was on Baron's Barracudas, one of the original Harold teams. He wrote and performed four reviews at the Second City (Chicago) where he received a Joseph Jefferson Award for Best Actor in a Review; has played at Steppenwolf and Goodman theaters, among others; and has many TV and film credits including *VEEP, Strangers with Candy, Boss, Angels and Demons,* and *Ice Harvest*. He is currently busy as the co-founder and co-artistic director of The Mission Theater in Chicago. David and TJ perform *TJ & Dave* regularly in Chicago and in New York, at the Barrow Street Theatre. *(Photo courtesy of Robert Adam Mayer)*

PAM VICTOR

Pam Victor gets to perform, write about, and teach improvisation for a living. She is the founding member of The Ha-Ha's and producer of *The Happier Valley Comedy Show*. She writes the *Geeking Out with ...* and *Zen of Improv* series as well as mostly true, mostly humorous essays on her blog *My Nephew is a Poodle*. She created and teaches the Zen of Improv Comedy and Mindfulness Through Laughter programs. Pam virtually lives at www.pamvictor.com. *(Photo by John A. Loos)*